Contents Page

Published by The British Publishing Company Limited © 2007.
The British Publishing Company Limited, 33 St Michaels Square, Gloucester GL1 1HX
www.british-publishing.com

Printed by Pensord, Tram Road, Pontllanfraith, Blackwood NP12 2YA.

ISBN 0-7140-3815-6

"to me a guide is
about creating an
awareness of what
a place has to offer"

Gloucester Introduction

I love history – all history. I presume that as you are reading these carefully chosen words you do too. Thank you for doing so.

I am totally aware that I am in a privileged position to have your eyes and attention even for a short amount of time. In this little book I will present to you my personal thoughts of the glories of Gloucester. I will never ever tell you what not to do or where to go, you must have that choice.

I will point out what enthuses me, paint a picture and place before you the facts and information of all that makes Gloucester unique to give you the opportunity to sample a piece of Gloucester heritage and life that tickles your fancy.

In a world bent on globalisation where retail centres, malls and many High Streets are full of the same choice, Hobson's choice, no choice of where to buy, drink or eat, it is history that gives a place its own peculiar brilliance and particular individual appeal. There is only ONE Gloucester Cathedral, thank God, but there are replica brands in a never-ending chain of the same quashing the exclusive charm and character of many beautiful places.

To me a guide is about creating an awareness of what a place has to offer. But far too many of them tell you to bypass this place or that as being 'not worth the stop'. Some cast aspersions on attractions or locations that proffer their own wee treasures that ARE worth the time and effort for you to make up your own mind. One person's rubbish could be your treasure.

This is a little book of discovery that lists what is on offer in one of Britain's greatest cities. I will present to you what pleases me and leave you to seek out what brings you joy or pleasure.

How can any one person or any one place please all the people all the time? I would say it's impossible. I hope my love and enthusiasm for places and their past will point you in the right direction to pursue your particular interest, obsession or hobby. It is pretty obvious that if you don't know if something is out there to go and visit then you will miss it! That is what this little guide book is all about, a compass to somewhere evocative and enjoyable that might spark off a brand new interest or trigger a desire for more historical exploration elsewhere.

I am very interested in your Gloucester thoughts whether you were born here, are resident within its city limits, passing through or a first-time or long-term visitor. I am always pleased to hear from you as you have taken the time to delight in this bright city.

For me, appreciating each chapter of a place's story since its origins means we can look forward with anticipation to what is to come, after all since you began reading this book everything you have read so far is now history.

Russell Grant

Russell Grant

Gloucester Origins

Let's start at the very beginning . . .

Around 5000 years ago (give or take a century) a couple of Celts – British to the Romans, you and me, Welsh to the Saxons – are foraging in virgin territory in what we now know as the Vale of Gloucester. From a distance they see a river, and as they search for a place to ford it one exclaims 'Gloyw!' which in the British tongue means, as it still does today (in Welsh), *'bright and shiny'*.

They had reached where the River Severn parts into three streams, or back in those days perhaps even more; maybe sunlight was rippling and glittering on the waters or perhaps some shiny object was magnified in the waters catching the sun's rays? Anyway, whatever caught their eye, from that moment on it became known as the bright or shiny place.

" imagine what your British ancestors first saw all those centuries ago "

There you have the first part of the place name of **GLOU**cester. Like all place names a journey had begun. But there is no evidence of a British village or place having been built there where the local population lived.

Around AD 48/49 the Roman 20th Legion built a fortress at Kingsholm not far from an iron-age settlement. They took the local name and from it **GLEVUM** was born, corrupted by the Latin lingo. It was in the reign of Emperor Marcus Cocceius Nerva (AD 96/98) that in AD 97 Gloucester became a Colonia, the highest ranking Roman city, and was named Colonia Nervia(na) Glevensium, shortened to **GLEVUM**. A Colonia was a sought-after Roman retirement city for old veterans or soldiers needing some R&R from being on duty probably at the border region of the British Kingdom of Gwent (Monmouthshire) and the Roman province of Britannia.

Some scholars suggest the name refers to *'famous, splendid or noble place'* perhaps due to the fort then occupying the area we call Kingsholm today: **HOLM** is Nordic and Germanic for a river island or plain by a river, hey presto we have the Isle of Alney, now a nature reserve. Excavations show evidence the Romans may have built up to five bridges to cross the many partings of the Severn.

The Brits had a word for forts and castles – **'CAER'** as in Caernarfon (the fort of Arfon). **'CAERGLOYW'**, or to be very British **'CAERLOYW'** as the **'G'** is dropped due to mutation: *the fort at the bright place*.

Nearly every clever school kid knows a town name ending in **'CASTER'** or **'CHESTER'** has some connection with the Roman occupation; as **CAER-GLOYW** grew it was to become the place of a great Roman colony and fortress as the local British called it.

Following the Romans the local Mercians (Anglo-Saxons) had their say by combining the British **(GLOYW)** and the description of the Roman fort with their own language (**CHESTER** alters to the simpler **CESTER** – taken from the Latin castra: a camp) and out came **GLOUCESTER:** *the Roman fort at the bright, shiny place!*

Mind you it was only at the beginning of the 9th century that the city's name was written as **GLOECESTER** and at a later date at the turn of that century, **GLEAWAN CEASTER**. This seems to be a wholesale invasion of the Anglo-Saxons who misinterpreted the British **'GLOYW'** and tried to highjack the whole name with their name **'GLEAW'**; they might look similar but the meaning – wise or prudent – is miles off the mark. It is so easy to get sucked into such corruptions.

Although the third stream has now disappeared, go for a walk by the River Severn or, as us Brits would call it, Afon Safren and from AD 550, Hafren. According to British legend Sabrina was the name of a princess who was drowned in the Safren or Severn. Was the river named after her or vice versa? It is also said Sabrina was a British goddess who lived there. Take your map and imagine what your British ancestors first saw all those centuries ago and gives **GLOUCESTER** its name today: *the bright city*.

"the second Gloucester Coat
of Arms was recorded in 1623"

SHOPPING

Gloucester Heraldry

Heralds were originally messengers empowered by the sovereign to be, amongst other things, in charge of granting and documenting Coats of Arms.

The College of Arms in London is the 'home' of the Royal Kings of Arms and it is only through the Head of the College, the Earl Marshall, a royal office holder appointed by the sovereign, that Coats of Arms can be petitioned and through Letter Patent can be officially granted.

Back in medieval times when heraldry was geared toward personal and family identity some of the great cities, London, Norwich and Gloucester, (*circa* 1200) placed in their adopted city seals heraldic shields, which in some cases remain their civic identity by prescriptive right, in other words as a result of long-standing custom or uninterrupted possession.

Gloucester's first seal bears a conventional representation of the city depicted as a triangular walled and battlement-enclosure with a square tower in the middle flanked by a circular bastion on each side. In the centre of the front wall is a double door with a circular window on each side and in the base are the waters of the River Severn.

During the 1500s and 1600s the Heralds, in the course of their nationwide travels called 'Visitations', recorded and sanctioned many of the arms adopted by different places – as was so with Gloucester in 1652.

The original Gloucester arms is known as the Tudor device granted in 1538 during the reign of Henry VIII. It is green with a gold pale charged with a sword in a blue scabbard studded with gold roundels, the hilt and pommel red, and upon its point a purple cap of maintenance with an ermine lining. On either side of the pale is a silver horseshoe and three nails with their points towards the shoe; the chief is parted palewise gold and purple (or red) and charged with a silver boar's head (sometimes quoted as having a red 'quince apple' in the mouth) between a red rose and a white rose, each halved with a golden sun with its rays streaming towards the boar's head.

The sword is that carried before the Mayor by authority of the charter granted by good King Richard III in 1483 – which created Gloucester a city and county in its own right; the horseshoes and nails stand for Gloucester's ancient trade in iron. The roses represent the Houses of York and Lancaster and the sun in splendour is connected to Yorkist King Edward IV. The boar is particularly associated, and remains so to this day, with his brother Richard III who, before his accession to the throne, was undoubtedly the most famous Duke of Gloucester ever.

The second Gloucester Coat of Arms was recorded in 1623 during Charles I's reign, although some historians believe it may have been a decade or so earlier when King James I/ VI, his dad, was monarch. Whenever it was, it became known as the Commonwealth device, for it was in 1652 when Oliver Cromwell ruled that the crest and supporters were added at the Herald's Visitation.

On the Restoration of the Monarchy in 1660, the crest and supporters of the Commonwealth Coat were declared null and void since they were granted during the republic. Gloucester didn't want to abandon the arms which had been assigned to them, besides they had been in use since the first Stuart kings of Britain – and it is likely that these particular arms could well have been floating around even before the Tudor device anyway.

The red chevronels (little chevrons!) are from the arms of the family Clare, Earls of Gloucester, and roundels (balls!) from the arms of the See of Worcester, with which the See of Gloucester was at one time united.

The grant of 1652 incorporated the shield with the addition of a crest comprising a lion looking directly at you emerging from a mural or castle-like crown, holding in his right paw a broadsword and in the left paw a trowel – heraldically this is connected with plasterers but it is possible this is a symbol of Gloucester's historic industry in iron. The supporters on either side are a lion holding in the right forepaw a broadsword proper; together with the motto *'Fides Invicta Triumphat'* (unconquered faith triumphs). The motto was adopted as a tribute to the spirit of the citizens of Gloucester who in 1643 successfully held the besieged city against the Royalist cavaliers in the Parliamentarian cause.

The Commonwealth Coat has been in continuous use ever since without serious challenge. To protect it legally Gloucester finally and formally decided to regularise the position by having the Coat recorded in the College of Arms and officially granted to them by Letter Patent dated 16th April 1945.

Where to see them!
On my walking tours of Gloucester I saw the Tudor Coat twice – once in the courtyard of the New Inn: go under the arch and look up towards the gallery straight ahead, up a bit and there it is. And surprisingly I also saw it on the modern fascia to the entrance of The Mall Eastgate shopping centre.

The Commonwealth Coat pops up everywhere, particularly on the clothing of stalwart supporters of Gloucester Rugby Football Club. In 2005 the club decided to dump this Coat as their historic badge and instead came up with a corporate logo that . . . well . . . judge for yourself. From 'proper' heraldry came two lions holding swords supporting a dark blue rugby ball with three red wiggles in a shield with a mural crown crest. What's that all about! The perpetrators would have done better to have put the ball and wiggles into a blank shield, or stuck with the status quo rather than a messy mix 'n' match and making a Gloucester Old Spot's ear of it. You know what; if something ain't broke, why fix it?

Royal Gloucester

The British and The Romans

AD 43: Togodumnus who led the British against the invading Romans is said to be buried in Gloucester.

AD 44–74: The founding of Gloucester, attributed to Arviragus, which according to Camden was renamed Claudiocestria when Emperor Claudius married his daughter Genissa to the British King Arviragus. Juvenal, poet of the period describes Arviragus as the Black Bull. It is said that Arviragus returned to Britain from Rome and established the royal line King Arthur descended from. Despite the Roman presence Gloucester always remained a powerful British stronghold. Arviragus was buried in Gloucester *circa* AD 67. The Gloucester City Museum & Art Gallery has an impressive array of Romano-British headstones and other awesome artefacts from this period.

AD 96: Colonia Nerviae (Nervia or Nerviana) Glevum founded as the place for Roman old boys and the battle-fatigued to put their feet up. This placed Gloucester as one of the cities at the very top of the Roman pecking order.

circa AD 180: British King Lucius buried in Gloucester. Lucius may have been real, he may have been myth; he may have been a Roman General who was seconded over to Brittany to quell the British revolt. British/Welsh tradition suggests Lucius was the paternal line to rulers of British kingdoms in Gwent (Monmouthshire), Powys (mid-Wales), Strathclyde (West of Scotland around Glasgow), Kernow (Cornwall) and Brittany.

circa AD 425–circa AD 466; circa AD 471–circa AD 480: King Vortigern Vorteneu. The British form of this is Gwrtheyrn Gwrtheneu (the Thin). Despite Vortigern sounding as though this is the King of Britain's name it is not, it is his title, as 'gern' means leader it is probable it derives from the northern British Tribes, such as the Picts. It means Over or High King. His real name (or that of his father or even grandfather) is either Vitalis (Gwidol in Welsh) or Vitalinus (Gwidolin). There is archaeological proof of his existence in the remains of a villa near Gloucester, this is consistent with the fact that his home area was along what we now call the Welsh borders. Vortigern Vitalis is said

to have spent most of his early years in Gloucester and is likely to have been its leader or king. His eldest son Vortimer ruled the British kingdom of Gwent (Monmouthshire). It is said his grandfather or great grandfather was the founder of Gloucester but his name appears long after Gloucester had been founded!

The Saxons

AD 577: The Independence of British Roman Gloucester was ended. The kings of Wessex who had been expansionist in their aims decided to invade and take over the area of the lower Severn valley. The Anglo-Saxon Chronicle records that Cuthwine and Ceawlin fought against the British and killed three kings, Commail, Condidan and Farinmail at Deorham (Dyrham) and took three cities from them, Gloucester, Cirencester and Bath.

It is likely that Commail was the last British King of Gloucester, and Ceawlin, King of Wessex, occupied and took Gloucester. On the day of this battle the British powerbase was driven even further west into Wales.

Gloucester was the hub of the kingdom of Hwicce (covering approximately Gloucestershire, Warwickshire and Worcestershire and very possibly extended into the City of Bath) which was a subkingdom to the greater Mercia. It had been the meat in the sandwich between the two great kingdom-states of Wessex and Mercia but was eventually merged with Mercia in 7th century although Camden says it was part of Mercia from AD 570.

Gloucester proved popular with Saxon kings mainly due to its strategic position between Mercia, Wessex and the British (known to the Saxons as Wales – land of the foreigners or strangers, cheek, the Saxons were that!). Saxon kings held councils and courts at Gloucester from the 9th century on.

In **AD 871** Alfred the Great gave Gloucester monetary and economic powers by establishing a city mint.

Summer **AD 877** – January **AD 878**: Gloucester was besieged and captured by the Danes. The Norse went south to Chippenham in Wiltshire where they raised the ire of their arch nemesis King Alfred who defeated them at the battle of Ethandun (Edington, Wiltshire).

In **AD 896** Alfred held his Great Witan in Gloucester – which accorded the city with a parliamentary power and importance.

Aethelred and Alfred's daughter Aethelflaed became the Great king's viceroy in the city and the couple made Gloucester their capital. It became and remained at the heart of the kingdom of Mercia.

Both Aethelred II of Mercia and Aethelflaed Lady of the Mercians had their palace at Kingsholm, Gloucester. They founded St Oswald's Priory where they were buried in **AD 911** and **AD 918**.

Between the death of her husband and her own demise, Aethelflaed helped transform Gloucester and put it at the very centre of her brilliant and successful campaigns against the Danes. She was buried in St Oswald's Priory and her resting place is said to be in the back garden of the house at the end of the row nearest the ruins!

King Athelstan, very often called the first proper King of England, spent his child-hood in the city and died in Gloucester **AD 939/940**.

On route to his death bed at Pucklechurch King Edmund passed through the city for the last and final time.

Queen Aelfigu was mutilated and murdered in the city around **AD 958**.

King Edwy was the eldest son of King Edmund I. After feuding with his brother Edgar he had to forfeit northern Wessex. He died in Gloucester under mysterious circumstances and was buried in the city in **AD 959**.

King Edgar kept up the Saxon tradition of holding Witans in the city. In **AD 968** he lived in the city for a short time but was he around to see the Danes ravage the city in AD 980?

The Vikings

1014: Ethelred the Unready was crowned in the Abbey.

In **1016** Edmund Ironside, after his defeat by the Danes at Assandun, came to Gloucester to recruit his forces and his battle with King Canute was peaceably settled not far from the city. It is said the Isle of Alney was the place they put pen to paper.

Gloucester was under Danish rule from 870 to 878 and 1016 to 1035 but there is no chronicle of any permanent Danish settlement.

Edward the Confessor favoured Gloucester over Oxford and visited the city many times. In November **1044** there was a meeting of the Saxon Witan (the King's Council), and again in 1051, 1052 and 1055 as he loved to spend Christmas in the city. It is said he wore his crown in Gloucester at Christmas, Winchester at Easter and Westminster at Whitsuntide. Each city played capital of the kingdom as there was no fixed capital city then.

At the 1044 Witan the queen's mother, Emma came under everyone's scrutiny. We think it is possible she was plotting with her second husband, Cnut, to restore the Danish dynasty. As a result King Edward left Gloucester with the great and powerful Godwin, Earl of Wessex, the equally prominent Leofric (husband of Lady Godiva or Godgifa of Coventry), the Earl of Mercia and Siward the Strong Earl of Northumbria, ferocious half-Dane and not someone to cross in the day let alone a dark night and they confiscated all of Emma's lands and treasures.

Gruffydd ap Llywelyn, king of the Britons of north Cymru (Wales), attacked the British in their southern strongholds and then Herefordshire and its cathedral. On receiving news of this the king arrived at Gloucester earlier than usual in **1055** and the future King Harold II was sent to intercept the marauding Brits. Peace terms were agreed and ratified by the Witan but in 1062 Gruffudd's hot British head got out of control again, this time Harold was told to put a stop to it once and for all. Gruffudd was brought to Gloucester in 1063 and presented to Edward as a Christmas gift!

A Northumbrian noble called Gospatrick was murdered in Gloucester in 1064; this was apparently trumped up by Harold's brother Tostig and ordered by his sister Queen Eadguth.

Don't you just love it when the old saying 'hell hath no fury like a woman scorned' turns out to be the real thing! Just before the conquest, the Lady Maud took a shine to one of the earliest Lords of Gloucester, Brictric alias Brictric Meaw, he spurned her but went even further and refused to marry her. As a woman of ambition and doubtless with the dark avenging angel urging her on she married none other than William the Conqueror himself, and one of her first acts was to get her husband to fling Brictric into prison and seize all his assets and estates for the crown. Lady Macbeth has nothing on Lady Maud.

The House of Normandy

1068 is probably the year Gloucester came under William the Conqueror's direct rule and the first year he visited, two years after the Battle of Hastings. The city was to become a particular favourite of the victorious invader. An early chronicle reads that William would visit Winchester at Easter, Westminster at Pentecost and Gloucester at Midwinter.

This is also the supposed year the Castle was planned and started to be built.

1072: At the Synod of Gloucester Lanfranc consecrated Peter, Bishop of Lichfield. Synods often met before or after Witan or in this case, Norman Parliament, as happened in 1081 and 1085, both in Gloucester.

1085 was a signal year in English history and it was Gloucester where the regal voice was clearly heard! The Anglo-Saxon Chronicle states: 'at midwinter the king was at Gloucester with his Witan and there held his court for five days; and afterwards the archbishop and his clergy had a Synod of three days . . . after this the king had a great council and a very deep speech with his Witan about this land, and how it was peopled and by what men: then he sent his men over all England in to every shire and caused to be ascertained how many hundred hides were in the shire, or what land the King himself had, and cattle within the land, or what dues he ought to have in twelve months from this shire.' The result of this deep speech between King and councillors, which took place in Gloucester (probably in an old building which formed part of the monastery, and known as the Long Workroom) was the compilation of Domesday Book – a unique work that no other country has. It is a record of the value and ownership of the Norman lands in England.

After spending Christmas in Gloucester in **1092**, William II Rufus was taken very ill in Alveston near Bristol in New Year 1093.

He was brought back to Gloucester. William repented all his ill deeds and vowed to make amends if he was spared. He was and didn't!

King Malcolm Cadmore of Scotland came to Gloucester on William's command and was given safe conduct to clear the air and come to an agreement about their respective kingdoms. But when Malcolm reached the city on 24th August it was decreed he paid homage to William as a Scottish subject. He accepted England's overlordship but protested that the only place the Scottish monarch would do homage to their English overlords would be on the borderlands. Malcolm went back home to Scotland totally put out and angry. The Scot invaded Northumberland in November but was killed by the Earl of the county.

1099: King William held his last court at Gloucester at Christmas. In 1100 a local monk predicted a violent death for Rufus just before he headed for Hampshire and guess what, he was killed whilst hunting in the New Forest – it was an accident, well so they say . . .

1100: The Castle was completed!

Henry I held occasional courts in the city. In 1114 his visit included grants of land to St Peter's Abbey. On 2nd February 1123, an Archbishop of Canterbury was elected – William of Corbeil, Prior of St Osyth, Essex was the chosen one.

1124: One of the leaders of the revolt against Henry I, Hugh de Montfort was captured and sent to Gloucester where he was kept in 'miserable bonds' in Gloucester Castle.

1130: Henry I found money to complete the keep of the city's castle.

1134: Robert (Curthose) of Normandy, Henry's brother and prisoner, died at Cardiff and was buried in St Peter's Abbey Church.

1136: Augustinian canons fled from Llanthony Priory in Monmouthshire to Gloucester for safety's sake.

King Stephen was escorted in procession to Kingsholm in May **1138**.

Milo of Gloucester advised Stephen's rival Empress Matilda to advance on Gloucester from Bristol; this she did around 15th October **1139**. Milo had gathered all kinds of provisions for the Empress so the city was in all respects prepared to resist an attack.

Stephen marched in the direction of Gloucester and captured a small castle which Milo had erected at South Cerney. From there Milo marched to Wallingford, Berkshire which had been blockaded and returned in triumph to his home city complete with prisoners.

After more battles between the two cousins, Matilda and Stephen, after the Battle of Lincoln he was taken prisoner and carried in fetters to Gloucester where on 9th February **1141** he was presented to Matilda. He was then sent to Bristol supposedly for life. But all did not work out for Matilda who got carried away with her new powers. Control freak perhaps? Certainly the good people of London thought so who gave her the thumbs down.

As a result she was soon on the run and accompanied by her faithful Milo was near to death through exhaustion and 'continued her journey as she had been a corpse strapped on her horse and carried into Gloucester'. Milo struggled on in her service trying to raise money to pay the troops from church funds for which he was excommunicated. He was killed in 1143 whilst hunting in the Forest of Dean where an arrow shot at a deer but strangely hit him! He was taken to Gloucester Castle where he died and was eventually buried in the Chapter House at Llanthony Priory Secunda, which he had founded.

What is odd about Milo is he offered his loyal services to Stephen and then when the Empress Matilda decided to fight for the throne he swapped sides. It is said that he made a promise to her father Henry I to support his daughter, which he did in fealty to the King.

The House of Plantagenet

From **1142** Henry Plantagenet lived in Gloucester between the ages of 9 and 14. On his return to the city at a later date when King Henry II, he fell head over heels for Fair Rosamunde from Frampton on Severn. As father of Richard the Lionheart, King John and Geoffrey of Anjou and married to the incredibly powerful Eleanor of Aquitaine, this relationship became a thorn in his romantic side and was used against Eleanor as a vicious weapon. Yet he could not live with Eleanor but could not live without her either – if only for her dowry of many French lands.

Henry II granted Gloucester its charter in the first year of his reign **1155** with the following words: 'Know ye that I have granted to my burgesses at Gloucester the same customs and liberties throughout my land of toll and of all other things as the citizens of London and those of Winchester ever had at any time in the time of King Henry, my grandfather.'

Henry II constructed the keep between cathedral and quay. He visited Gloucester in **1175** as he did all important towns in his kingdom to restore peace after underlying unrest when he was in Normandy. In Gloucester the order barons and British princes swore fidelity to him and safety of the Marches was assured. In the June he held a conference on British (Welsh) affairs.

1188: The dysfunctional family of Henry and Eleanor were at it again when their younger son, John, wooed Hadwisa, daughter of Earl William of Gloucester. A happy ending? What do you think, perhaps her title had something to do with it . . . read on.

1194: Richard I granted Gloucester a charter the same as those conferred by Henry II.

21st April **1200:** King John granted Gloucester a charter. That same year, whilst in the city, he offered safe conduct to William, King of Scotland.

King John imprisoned his first wife in Gloucester Castle where she remained for the rest of her life. He married her for her titles, she being the daughter of the Earl of Gloucester.

King John held court at Gloucester, maintaining several royal galleys on the Severn after 1204.

Shortly before he died John was at Gloucester trying to repress a rebellion at his constant breaking of Magna Carta he had signed at Runnymede. John retreated to Gloucester in the face of a revolt amongst his French mercenaries. He was joined by Gualo, the Pope's legate. John died on 19th October.

1216: Henry III crowned at Gloucester. At nine years old the youngster had to be crowned post haste and the ceremony took place on 28th October in the cathedral. It is said the Earl of Pembroke and Marshal of England pleaded on the boy's behalf not to visit the sins of the father (King John) upon the son, but to loyally support the young king and aid in the expulsion of the foreigner who was striving to dispossess him of his inheritance. The coronation ceremony was not an imposing one, as owing to the speed with which it had been arranged there was only a small attendance of barons and bishops. Moreover Stephen Langton, Archbishop of Canterbury, having been suspended by the Pope for this loyal opposition to the tyranny of John, was precluded from officiating. According to the official account, his place was taken by Gualo the legate, but there seems some doubt whether the ceremony was not performed by the Archbishop of Dublin or Bishop of Winchester. Langton's substitute, whoever he was, placed on the king's head a plain circular band of gold, probably his mother's bracelet or torque because his father, King John, had lost the crown jewels in the Wash off the north-west coast of East Anglia. He was made to swear before the high altar, the good book, gospels and relics that he would rule constitutionally and broadcast to the world how his father had subjected the nation to humiliation. Mass was then held followed by merry-making.

1227: Henry III confirmed John's charter for Gloucester.

It is said that Gloucester and Winchester were Henry III's favourite places but he didn't appear to be particularly generous to Gloucester and tended to visit out of necessity rather than choice.

14th August **1233:** Henry III summoned all who owed him military service. The Earl of Pembroke was declared a traitor and went into south Wales to ravage the lands with his Poitevin mercenaries. He returned to Gloucester on 2nd November to declare the city as centre of operations against the insurgent barons. On 11th November the king met with a reverse in fortunes. His camp was plundered and he returned to Gloucester where he remained till after Christmas; he left early in 1234. He returned 29th May to hold a parliament to which all the revolting barons were summoned where he granted them a free pardon.

In **1241** Henry III headed for Llanthony Secunda Priory where he conducted affairs of state in the July.

In **1263** the king appointed a French Knight, Matthew de Besille, to be Constable of the City and Sheriff of the County but the local nobles didn't want a Frenchman and declared their own man William Tracy, from Gloucestershire, as the man.

Simon de Montfort got involved and after a few days' siege took Gloucester Castle and made De Besille his prisoner. Prince Edward eventually outsmarted de Montfort to take back Gloucester.

Henry collected his army at Gloucester in **1222** to march to Wales and take on the Great Llywelyn; battles took place in 1228 and 1231. In 1240, the year of Llywelyn's death, Henry III chose Gloucester as the site where his son Dafydd ap Llywelyn paid him homage in the May. But in 1241 Dafydd decided to take on Henry, only to submit at Shrewsbury when opposed by Henry at the head of an army gathered, once more, at Gloucester.

Early May **1265**: Henry III and his son Edward I were constrained at Gloucester Castle by Simon de Montfort before the battle at Evesham where De Montfort met his doom.

Remember this rhyme?
Doctor Foster went to Gloucester
In a shower of rain;
He stepped in a puddle,
Right up to his middle,
And never went there again.

It is odd that this rhyme is attributed to King Edward I who was around between 1239 and 1307 for there is no record of it before Queen Victoria in 1844! It refers to a forgettable royal visit to the city when the roads were so bad that King Ted, his horse and retinue got stuck in the mud and the ruinous roads were so full of pot holes he said he would never return to Gloucester again until they had sorted out the state of the roads!

Edward I confirmed Gloucester's charter and rights to hold a fair from 23rd to 29th June each year.

According to my research he did came to Gloucester again on 28th September **1274** in a jaw-jaw with Llywelyn ap Gruffudd Prince of Wales asking for the British Prince's allegiance.

In the summer of 1278 the Statutes of Gloucester Parliament was held. In 1281 the King, Edward I, commissioned Peter Corbet to destroy wolves in Gloucestershire. They were to defuse the tyranny of the barons and increase the revenue of the Crown – break down the feudal courts and give the king's justice a wider range and in reach of all. In 1301 Parliament met again in Gloucester.

Edward II came to Gloucester in spring **1321** from 26th March to 16th April to deal with the growing hassle from across the border in Wales. On his final day he went to the Franciscans' house. On 5th and 13th April he asked unhappy nobles to join him and put down any discontent or face punishment. He was ignored and not feeling secure where 'so many discontented noblemen and commons being so near' he left for Bristol. In **1322** he came back from 7th to 18th February and while there were writs for the recall of his favourites, the Despensers, he went to battle, won, came back and allowed the despised Despensers to take control of royal affairs. This resulted in a serious rift between Edward and his wife, Queen Isabella – he returned to the city again and again during the next few months. The queen went to France on the ruse she wanted to visit her brother the King of France in 1325 but by 1326 she was back at the head of an army determined to rid herself and family of the Despensers whom she blamed for coming between her husband and herself in every intimate way.

The king was deserted by his own army and friends and fled from London with Hugh Despenser, his particular favourite, and arrived at Gloucester on 10th and 11th October to try and raise an army – in his dreams! He even tried to reach Lundy Island by boat but the weather thwarted him. The queen, now aided and abetted by her own lover Roger Mortimer, headed for Gloucester and on 15th October she entered the city and was joined by an army from the north.

Edward III, Richard II and Henry V all came to Edward's tomb as pilgrims. In 1390 Richard flew into the city after hearing reports of fantastic miracles happening at his royal ancestor's tomb.

Edward III was in Gloucester with his mum in October 1326 and 1328 and 29 when he appointed Lord Maurice of Berkeley, Governor of Gloucester Goal.

10th October **1326**: Edward III visited Gloucester. He confirmed Gloucester's charter and relieved citizens from inflationary hikes of the ferm or rents.

1349: Black Death haunted the city.

20th October to 16th November **1378**: Richard II's Parliament. His uncle, John of Gaunt, Duke of Lancaster, unpopular in London for many reasons including increasing taxes on wine and wanting to lessen the powers of the City of London itself, chose Gloucester to hold a Parliament of the young king. Business began daily at 8am. The ruinous wars in France had left the king's coffers empty but the MPs were in no mood to give him more money to squander when they had already given him more money than had ever been raised in so short a time and refused to give in. There were other laws passed including the Statute of Labourers and this became the tinder box of the Wat Tyler rebellion in 1381.

She gave back Berkeley Castle to Thomas Maurice (it having been snatched by the king from the rightful owner to give to the Despensers!) on her way to Bristol. On 16th November Edward was taken by his enemies at Bristol Castle and imprisoned at Berkeley where he was murdered or some people said he escaped. The story is in the Cathedral zone of the book.

Edward II became one of Gloucester's great attractions. He was buried in the Cathedral (then St Peter's Abbey) because Malmesbury and Bristol Abbeys are said to have refused to bury the murdered king in their grounds. Interestingly his heart is said to have been buried with that of his scorned wife who with her lover Roger Mortimer took on her husband during his reign and was responsible for his demise. Did Edward have the last laugh with his heart in her coffin in Greyfriars Church, Newgate? Or was his heart hers all the time?

His tomb became the centre of a martyr cult and when his son Edward III succeeded him to the throne, he had his father's tomb decorated so magnificently that the ordinary people who came and prayed thought they were in the presence of a saint.

Richard II stayed at Gloucester Castle in **1378** but the city was so crowded that the monks had to camp in their orchard so that the clerics could be accommodated in the Abbey and Llanthony Priory. In fact the green in the cloisters was 'trampled down with wrestling and football'! As if that wasn't enough the king borrowed £40 from Gloucester to pay for the supplies used, as what he received from Parliament wasn't sufficient! He did the same in 1397 borrowing £200. I couldn't find out if he ever paid the city back.

Richard II confirmed Gloucester's charter but along with Worcester was required to pay for the cost of a small balinger warship.

Henry IV paid a flying visit to Gloucester in **1403** on his way to Bristol to assert his authority over the Welsh/British. In 1407 he held Parliament in the city as London had the plague and he needed the fresh air of the country, and Gloucester was it. From 20th October to 2nd December the Commons occupied the refectory of the Abbey. A French Ambassador visited the city: he had been sent to arrange a truce and sign a treaty on 9th December to bring the dying war between England and France to a close. It was at this council that he began a change in law by bringing public finance under Parliamentary scrutiny and control.

Henry IV confirmed Gloucester's charter with the rights to charge import duty on certain goods.

Henry V visited Llanthony Priory in **1415**. Parliament was assembled in Gloucester on 15th February 1420 but after a fortnight was adjourned to Westminster, Middlesex.

Edward, Earl of March was in Gloucester when he heard his father, the Duke of York, had been killed and the Yorkists defeated at the Battle of Wakefield, 30th December **1460**. He raised an army of 30,000 men with which he defeated the Lancastrians under Jasper Tudor at Mortimer's Cross in Herefordshire on 2nd February 1461. Edward was proclaimed king in the March but the Yorkists were not yet invincible. In 1463 Queen Margaret fled from England. In 1464 Henry VI was captured and imprisoned in the Tower of London. After more battles and defeats the queen headed towards the Tudors' native Wales to raise an army. The Yorkist Governor of Gloucester closed the city gates to Queen Margaret and her son Edward in 1471 denying them a crossing of the Severn and forcing them to go to Tewkesbury. This one act is said to have lost them the war.

In contrast Edward IV was allowed in as he rode to Tewkesbury for the battle of all battles against her.

Edward IV in the first year of his reign created his young brother Richard (later the III) Duke of Gloucester and granted him £65 rent (ferm) that was payable by the city. Richard thanked the city when he became king on 6th July 1483 by granting it a Charter of Incorporation on 2nd September **1483** that made Gloucester a city and county in its own right, enlarging its municipal privilege and shifting its boundaries, adding the ancient hundred of Dudston and King's Barton which took the city's powers as far south as almost to Stroud, north to Hatherley and east to Brockworth. And good old Dick refused £40 of his city rents. At his own coronation in 1483 on reaching Gloucester in August the burgesses offered him a gift to help pay for his nationwide progress but he declined to take it, saying he would rather have the hearts of the people of Gloucester than their money.

In **1485** refugees headed into Gloucester's St John's Church after the Battle of Bosworth and Richard's demise.

The House of Tudor

In 1485, the first year of his reign, Henry VII made progress through his kingdom and came to Gloucester. In March 1486 he left London, went to York and turned south-west, reaching Gloucester the Friday after Whitsunday. He was met three miles outside the city gates by 'the Mayor, Sheriff and other people in great number in red gowns and all on horseback' as the chronicle of the day announced. It continued, 'processions of friars and clergy welcomed him between the two bridges and at the door of St Peters Abbey he was received by William Farley, the abbot and his monks'. He stayed till the Monday and then headed to Bristol.

The city asked him to continue King Richard's generosity in returning £40 of the rents, to which the prudent Henry told them to come to London when he could consider it in his leisure time – a polite way of saying NO, methinks! In September **1491** he made several visits to Llanthony Priory. Between 19th December **1500** and 26th August **1501** he stayed for 28 days, it is said for medical reasons.

1489: Henry VII confirmed Gloucester's charter but did not give back to the city the £40 the ferm or rents as reduced by Richard III but kept it at £65 – and wanted every penny!

Henry VIII and Anne Boleyn visited the city in July **1535**, Anne had been crowned queen two years earlier but Henry was already getting bored with her. The couple were afforded the same welcome as his father had been given years earlier. The mayor, according to custom, gave the mace to the king who returned it, which was symbolic of delivering the surrender of the city's franchises into the king's hands and their restitution. At Whitefriars they were welcomed by more noble ecclesiastics. The royals left on 7th August and were escorted by the Mayor and corporation as far as Quedgeley Green.

Henry VIII and his son Edward VI confirmed Richard III's city charter.

11th July **1553**: Lady Jane Grey was proclaimed Queen in accordance to Edward VI's will and dying wish. The royal herald announced this to the citizens of Gloucester from the gallery of The New Inn. Nine days later Mary Tudor took back the throne as hers by right leaving Lady Jane to face the axe.

When the Catholics regained power through Mary Tudor's sovereignty, Bishop Hooper of Gloucester was one of their first victims. Before Mary had been on the throne two months he was thrown, without trial, into the Fleet prison, where he remained for 18 months. Whilst in prison he said that he was used 'worse and more vilely than the veriest slave'. On 15th March 1554, he was stripped of his bishopric and on 22nd January 1555 he was tried in the Church of St Mary Overy, Southwark for heresy. He was not allowed to speak in his own defence but was offered the Queen's mercy if he would recant his Protestant beliefs. This he refused to do, and on the following morning he was sentenced to be burned as 'an obstinate, false and detestable heretic' in the city 'which he had infected with his pernicious doctrine' – which was Gloucester. He was sent back to Gloucester where he arrived on 7th February and was placed in the custody of the Sheriff, who treated him with 'more kindness than he had received at the hands of the keepers of the bishop's prison'.

He was visited by Sir Anthony Kingston who having given a homily on the sweetness of life and the bitterness of death, besought him, with tears in his eyes, to purchase pardon by recantation. Hooper answered him firmly but kindly that he could not – *'Well my Lord'* said Sir Anthony *'then there is no remedy, and I will take my leave. I thank God that ever I knew you, for God appointed you to call me, being a lost child.'* Hooper's execution took place on 9th February 1555 in St Mary's Square outside Gloucester Cathedral where his statue now stands. His sufferings were terribly protracted for owing to the dampness of the wood, the fire went out and had to be relit twice. He endured excruciating agony with unbelievable courage for nearly one hour before his spirit passed away.

Philip and Mary attempted to reduce the city's charter rights – the attempt failed.

Elizabeth I confirmed previous charters in **1561** and granted additional privileges.

Elizabeth I spent just one day in August (either 8th or 10th) at Gloucester in **1574**. In **1580** Elizabeth created Gloucester a Port complete with all trappings. In 1592 Elizabeth popped into the city again whilst spending time at Sudeley Castle.

The House of Stuart

In **1604** the plague hit Gloucester and carried off much of the population.

James I in **1605** by a charter related that 'our City of Gloucester is very ancient and populous' and changed the style of incorporation to 'the Mayor and Burgesses of the City of Gloucester in the County and City of Gloucester'.

1627: Charles I confirmed previous charters and their boundaries. During his reign Charles imposed a tax for coastal

defence on the people of Gloucester – one reason why the city stood for Parliament against the monarch when the British Civil War broke out in 1643. I suppose he got confused by the fact his cousin Elizabeth had created it a port in her reign even though it was miles away from the coast!

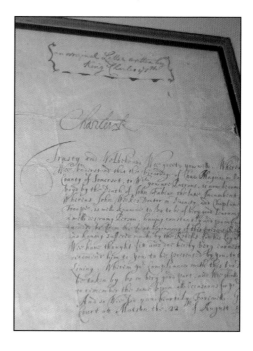

A handwritten letter by Charles I can be seen and read at the Gloucester Folk Museum. I found it spellbinding that this king who was later beheaded had written this letter personally in ink at such an important period in British history, and it was there in front of me. This is my kind of history. Wonderful!

Gloucester supported Cromwell and Parliament and resisted a siege by Charles I 10th August to 5th September **1643**. On hearing of the approach of the Earl of Essex and the London and Middlesex militia the king abandoned the siege late on 5th September – which became known as Gloucester Day.

Gloucester's walls were levelled by a vengeful Charles II (son of the murdered Charles I) and he razed the castle, which is now HM Prison.

In **1664** Charles II granted the city a charter which had to be surrendered in 1672, and then granted a new one which shrank its boundaries as confirmed by his father, exacting more revenge for Gloucester's Puritanism and in his eyes, taking a traitor's stance, by reducing the city's space to what it was before Richard III added the Hundred of Dudston and King's Barton, which by an Act of Parliament was taken away from Gloucester and transferred back to the county.

James II visited Gloucester briefly in August **1687** in an effort to increase his dwindling popularity; he received the sword of office and cap of maintenance at the south gate. He proceeded to St Edward's Gate where the Dean welcomed him. He spent two nights at the Deanery. As a Roman Catholic he attended Mass in a room over the Sheriff's Court in the Tolsey which forever after became known as the King's Chapel. As a city with a strong puritan background Gloucester had been strongly Parliamentarian in the Civil War; to spend all that money on a royal visit must have stuck in their craw. James left on 24th August.

In **1788** Hanoverian King George III came to town with Queen Charlotte and their children.

Prinny came to Gloucester in **1807** – known also as the Prince Regent, he was given the freedom of the city and was entertained at the King's Head, Westgate Street by the city council.

On 29th September **1849**, Queen Victoria visited Gloucester and was presented with a carpet for her personal use (why?). Being a woman who knew what she liked she offered it for sale to the public at a later date.

Not put off by the thought of another rug on 30th August **1852** Queen V had to change trains at Gloucester as she went on her way to Osborne House. The station was decorated but she didn't stay long enough to accept baubles, bangles or beads.

Edward Prince of Wales visited the Royal Agricultural Society's Show on the Oxleaze, Gloucester and granted royal patronage to the Infirmary on Southgate Street. It's hard work being royal – that was all on just one day, phew – 23rd June **1909**.

King George VI and Queen Elizabeth boosted morale with a trip to Gloster Aircraft in February **1940**.

3rd May **1955**, Queen Elizabeth II and Prince Philip celebrated Gloucester's 800-year-old anniversary of its first charter given by Henry II. In **1979** their daughter, the Princess Royal, reopened Ladybellegate House, it having been refurbished by the excellent Gloucester Civic Trust.

In **1986**, Queen Elizabeth opened the new Widden Street Primary School in the city on 14th April a few days before her birthday and on 6th November **1990** Charles, Prince of Wales, visited Gloucester a few days before his birthday!

Easter **2003** and Gloucester Cathedral was the setting for the traditional Maundy Thursday distribution of silver coins to specially chosen pensioners by Her Majesty, the Queen.

Gloucester Titles

Dukes of Gloucester

Thomas of Woodstock, Duke of Gloucester from 1385
(born in Woodstock, Oxfordshire 7th January 1355 died 8th (or 9th) September 1397) Thomas was the thirteenth and youngest child of King Edward III of England and Queen Philippa. He was the king's lieutenant in France but lost face when he failed to take Nantes against a combined French and Castilian army in 1380.

After becoming Duke of Gloucester whilst taking the high road to Scotland he became head of the anti-Richard Lords Appellant and de facto controller of Richard II's government. He decided that the royal advisers be removed forthwith. He secured a conviction of treason of all the king's counsellors at what became known as the Merciless Parliament in 1388, finding them all guilty of living in vice and deluding the king. Thanks to John of Gaunt, the following May Richard II regained power and he and his uncle the Duke of Gloucester made peace and together went across the seas to Ireland in 1394.

In 1397 Gloucester was arrested by the king himself at Pleshey Castle in Essex from where he was taken to Calais and murdered on the orders of his nephew, Richard. Before he could appeal, he was declared a traitor in similar vein to how he had disposed of the royal advisers years before. His death caused outcry amongst the nobility and added to Richard's unpopularity. His daughter was known as Anne of Gloucester although the title became forfeit on his murder in 1397.

Humphrey, Duke of Gloucester from 1414 'Good Duke Humphrey'
(born 1390 died 23rd February 1447) was the fifth son of King Henry IV of England by his first wife, Mary de Bohun. His brother Henry V succeeded to the throne and Humphrey fought for Harry, Crispin and St George and was wounded at the famous Battle of Agincourt in 1415. On the death of Henry V he became regent of the kingdom and protector to his young nephew, King Henry VI. But his brother's will made it clear that on his death the regency should go to Gloucester's older brother John of Lancaster, to which Parliament concurred.

Around about 1422 he married Jacqueline, Countess of Hainault and Holland, daughter of William VI. The marriage was annulled in 1428, and Jacqueline died – disinherited – in 1436. Meanwhile, amidst building criticism Gloucester remarried, his second wife being his former mistress, Eleanor Cobham.

In 1441, Eleanor was tried and convicted of practising magic against King Henry VI in an attempt to help Gloucester to succeed to the throne, as he was now heir presumptive. She died in prison. Following his wife's conviction, Gloucester himself was arrested on a charge of treason. He died, or was assassinated, at Bury St Edmunds, Suffolk whilst in custody a few days later.

This particular Duke of Gloucester was indecisive, had little or no staying power and was unable to finish things he started. His name lives on in 'Duke Humfrey's Library', the duke having left a gift of books, which form the heart of the Bodleian Library in Oxford.

Richard III became Duke of Gloucester in 1461

(born at Fotheringhay Castle, Northamptonshire, 2nd October 1452 died 22nd August 1485) and was probably the most famous or notorious holder of the title, dependent upon your point of view. He was one of the few Dukes of Gloucester who did something for the city.

Richard was king from 1483 until his death, and he conferred upon the city in his coronation year its charter making it a city and county in its own right. It confirmed the 1155 Henry I charter of incorporation but with a little bit extra! After the demise of his brother King Edward IV, Richard briefly governed as the Lord Protector for Edward's son King Edward V but cunningly placed Edward and his brother Richard in the Tower of London and crowned himself king on 6th July 1483.

Two large-scale rebellions rose against Richard. The first, in 1483, was led by his own 'kingmaker', Henry Stafford, Duke of Buckingham. The revolt was not successful and Buckingham was executed at Salisbury. However, in 1485, a more formidable enemy took arms against Richard, headed by the formidable Welshman/Briton Henry Tudor, 2nd Earl of Richmond (later King Henry VII). At this point all Richard's enemies allied and the king was killed at the Battle of Bosworth Field, Leicestershire. He was the last monarch from the House of York, the last Plantagenet king, and last English king to die in battle – and his death at the Battle of Bosworth ended the Wars of the Roses and introduced the iconic Tudors to the throne.

Henry Stuart, Duke of Gloucester from 1659

(born in Oatlands Park, Weybridge, Surrey, 8th July 1640 died 18th September 1660) was the son of Charles I and Queen Henrietta Maria. After his father's defeat at the end of the British Civil War, the six-year-old prince (unlike his older brothers, who escaped with their mother to France), was captured and brought to the royal apartments in the White Tower of the Tower of London, under the 'protection' of the republican army. It was even suggested that the young prince be placed on the throne as a puppet with Oliver Cromwell and parliament pulling the strings. It was thought he was young enough not to have been 'corrupted' by the Catholic and absolutist views of his mother and father. This never came to pass. Eventually, in 1652, republican leader Oliver Cromwell agreed to release him, and he was sent to join his mother and brothers in Paris.

Cromwell's influence did take hold as Henry had become a staunch Protestant. His doctrine clashed vehemently with his mother's and they quarrelled so much over matters of religion and politics that their mutual dislike led to Henrietta virtually expelling him from her presence, and he went to join the Spanish armies fighting at Dunkirk. He returned to Britain as part of his brother Charles II's triumphant restoration ride through London in May 1660. He was created Duke of Gloucester by him but died suddenly of smallpox not long afterwards.

Decades later, during the exclusion crisis Henry was looked back on as a kind of 'lost leader', as what might have been a legitimate, warlike, Protestant alternative to the equally unpalatable choices of either James II or the Duke of Monmouth.

Queen Anne's Little Duke of Gloucester

Prince William

(born 24th July 1689 died 29th July 1700)
The only child out of the 18 Queen Anne gave birth to, to live beyond infancy, Prince William was declared by his uncle, the then king, William III, to be Duke of Gloucester at his birth on 24th July 1689, but no formal documentation for such a creation exists. He died on 29th July 1700.

Prince Frederick Louis

(born in Hanover, Germany, 1st February 1707 died at Leicester House, London 31st March 1751) George II's heir apparent and father of George III. There is no formal documentation for his creation as Duke of Gloucester.

Prince William Henry, Duke of Gloucester from 1764

(born at Leicester House London, 14th November 1743 died 25th August 1805)
His father was the Prince Frederick, Prince of Wales, eldest son of King George II and Caroline of Ansbach. His mother was the Princess of Wales (née Augusta of Saxe-Gotha). Prince William Henry joined the British Army. His elder brother King George III became king on 25th October 1760 and four years later created William Henry Duke of Gloucester. Gloucester, Ontario is named in his honour.

HRH Prince William Frederick, Duke of Gloucester from 1805

(born in Rome, Italy, 15th January 1776 died 30th November 1834) His father was Prince William Henry, Duke of Gloucester, the third son of the Prince of Wales.

His mother was Maria, Duchess of Gloucester, the illegitimate daughter of Edward Walpole and granddaughter of Robert Walpole, the great and first British Prime Minister. On 25th August 1805, Prince William's father died, and he inherited the title Duke of Gloucester.

HRH Prince Henry, Duke of Gloucester from 1928

(born at York Cottage, Sandringham, Norfolk, 31st March 1900 died 10th June 1974) His father was Prince George, Duke of York (later King George V), his mother the Duchess of York (later Queen Mary). In 1898, Queen Victoria issued letters patent granting the children of the Duke and Duchess of York the style Royal Highness.

In 1928, his father, by now King George V, created him Duke of Gloucester. On 2nd November 1930 he attended the coronation of Haile Selassie of Ethiopia in Addis Ababa. In 1934, King George V as King of Ireland made him a Knight of St Patrick (KP), Ireland's chivalric order. It was the last time this order was ever awarded.

Returning to the UK, the Duke and Duchess of Gloucester lived at Barnwell Manor in Northamptonshire with an apartment in Kensington Palace. The Duke attended the coronation of his niece, Queen Elizabeth, in 1953. In 1972, the Duke's eldest son, Prince William, tragically died in a plane crash. The Duke was the last surviving child of the late King and Queen. When he died on 10th June 1974 his second eldest son, Prince Richard, inherited the title of Duke of Gloucester. The old Duke's wife, Alice, received permission from Queen Elizabeth II to be styled Princess Alice, Duchess of Gloucester to distinguish herself from Prince Richard's wife. She survived until

2004, and at the age of 102 became the longest-lived member of the British Royal Family in history.

HRH Prince Richard, Duke of Gloucester from 1974

(born on 26th August 1944 at Barnwell Manor in Northamptonshire) His father was Prince Henry, Duke of Gloucester; his mother was Alice, Duchess of Gloucester. At the time of his birth, he was second in line to his father's Dukedom, behind his brother, Prince William of Gloucester.

When he was four months old, Prince Richard accompanied his parents to Australia, where his father was Governor-General from 1945 to 1947. The family returned to Britain in 1947. After university and completing his training, he went into practice as a partner in a firm of London architects. Although he planned to practise full time as an architect, the unforeseen death of his brother, Prince William of Gloucester, left Richard first in line to his father's Dukedom. He therefore resigned his partnership, and began to represent his cousin, Queen Elizabeth II, on Royal occasions. On 8th June 1972, Prince Richard of Gloucester married Birgitte van Deurs, a Danish woman, at St Andrew's Church in his home village of Barnwell.

On 10th June 1974, Prince Richard's father died and he succeeded to the title Duke of Gloucester. The Duke is particularly interested in architecture and conservation. A keen motorist, Prince Richard was president of the Institute of Advanced Motorists for 32 years. The Duke and Duchess of Gloucester's official residence is at Kensington Palace and they have leased Barnwell Manor since 1994.

Earls of Gloucester

Earl or Jarl (Nordic) is an Anglo-Saxon and Norse title. It means the chieftain and it referred especially to the head honchos given an area to rule in a king's stead. In the Viking kingdoms, it became obsolete in the Middle Ages but in Britain, it is on a par with the continental count; same meaning, different root. An earl is a member of the British peerage and ranks below a marquess and above a viscount. The wife of an earl is a countess.

Before the Norman Conquest Earldoms of Gloucester covered a much wider area than just Gloucester or its shire. The earliest Earls or Jarls of Gloucester were probably Brictric, son of Algar, alias Brictric Meaw, and more certainly Swein, eldest son of Godwin, Earl of Kent and elder brother of Harold II who was killed at Hastings in 1066. In medieval times, the blurring of any distinction between the county town, in this case Gloucester, and county, Gloucestershire, when conferring earldoms was intended to make the titleholder governor of both city and county.

It is supposed that **William FitzEustace became 1st Earl of Gloucester in its first creation in 1093** *(died 1094)* After the Conquest it is possible that the Earldom of Gloucester was held by either William FitzEustace, perhaps the son of Eustace II Count of Boulogne. **Robert Fitzhamon** *(born between 1045–1055 and died in Falaise, Normandy, March 1107)*, Sieur de Creully in the Calvados region of Normandy, was Lord of Gloucester, not to be confused with the earldom – the 'Lord' here most probably refers to Lord of the Manor. Fitzhamon is sometimes called Earl of Gloucester, but was never so created formally and calling him so is probably due to the confusion of his being Lord of Gloucester.

He was allegedly grandson of Hamo Dentatus, the toothy or buck-toothed; as a kinsman of the Conqueror and one of the few Anglo-Norman barons to remain loyal to two successive kings Rufus and Henry I Beauclerc, he was a prominent figure in England and Normandy. However, not much is known about his earlier life or his exact relationship to William I and William II (William Rufus), but it is supposed they were cousins.

During the rebellion of 1088, he supported Rufus and was rewarded with great estates in Gloucestershire some of which belonged to the Empress Matilda. Fitzhamon married *circa* 1087–1090 Sibyl of Montgomery. His eldest daughter Mabel inherited his great estates and married *circa* 1119 Robert, 1st Earl of Gloucester. Fitzhamon's Gloucestershire property thus became the nucleus of the Earldom of Gloucester later given to his son-in-law.

He founded Tewkesbury Abbey in 1092. The abbey was apparently built under the influence of his wife Sibyl, said to be a beautiful and religious woman like her sisters. In 1105, he went to Normandy and was captured whilst fighting near his ancestral estates near Bayeux. This was one of the reasons King Henry I crossed the channel with a substantial force to rescue Robert later that year. Fitzhamon was freed, and joined Henry's campaign, which proceeded to besiege Falaise. There Fitzhamon was severely injured in the head; although he lived two more years, he was never the same mentally.

He is buried in the Chapter House at Tewkesbury Abbey, which he had founded and considerably enriched during his lifetime.

William FitzRobert, 2nd Earl of Gloucester from 1121
(born 23rd November 1116 – 1121 has also been suggested – died 23rd November 1183)
William married Hawise de Beaumont of Leicester. Because his only son and heir Robert died in 1166, Earl William made John Lackland, the younger son of King Henry II, heir to his earldom, if the king promised that John marry one of the earl's daughters (if the Church would allow it, they being related in the third degree). Until then the three sisters, Mabel FitzRobert of Gloucester, Amicia FitzRobert, Countess of Gloucester who was born in Tewkesbury in 1160, and Isabel, born in Gloucester in 1170, were to become co-heirs of the earldom. Isabel was known as Isabel of Gloucester and eventually had her own creation as Countess of Gloucester.

Isabel became Countess of Gloucester in its 3rd creation in 1186 *(born 1170 died 14th October 1217)* and King John Lackland became Earl of Gloucester in 1199
(born 1167 died 1216) when the title merged with the crown after he divorced Isabel. Isabel of Gloucester, the youngest daughter of William and Hawise, married King John when he was just Earl of Cornwall on 29th August 1189 at Marlborough, Wiltshire. A new title created in 1186 made her Countess of Gloucester. She never became Queen as John had their marriage annulled by the Pope; no doubt he wanted the title and knew it would become his, as they had no heirs. The official reason was they were too closely related being second cousins and it was a sin! As this was known all the time presumably it was a means to an end for John to grab as many of Isabel's possessions and titles as possible. She lost two titles as a result, Queen, and Countess of Gloucester.

John her ex-husband took the Gloucester title as it was merged with the Crown. Isabel did find literary fame as a witch in *The Devil and King John* by Philip Lindsay and just to confuse she was known under one of her other identities of Hadwisa in the Robin Hood stories. And if that isn't confusing enough, in some historical documents she is also known as Hawise, Joan, Eleanor, Avise and Avisa. Would the real Isabel of Gloucester sort herself out please!

Important note: It is the de Clares or Clares that gave their family coat of arms to the City of Gloucester's Coat of Arms.

Gilbert de Clare,
1st Earl of Gloucester from 1218
(born 1180 died 25th October 1230)
inherited the Clare estates from his mother Amice FitzRobert. In 1202, Gilbert was entrusted with the safekeeping of Harfleur and Montrevilliers in Normandy. They were at the vanguard of the powerhouse forces against King John in the Baronial wars that led to the signing of the Magna Carta, where Gilbert, the Earl of Gloucester was present.

He fought against the British (Welsh) and then joined a military expedition to Brittany (where the British/Welsh that left Britain due to Anglo-Saxon and Norman incursions had settled) but died on his way back home and was taken to Tewkesbury where he was interred.

Richard de Clare,
2nd Earl of Gloucester
(born 4th August 1222 died 15th July 1262 near Canterbury, Kent) was known as Strongbow due to his Irish successes. First, he fought against the British (Welsh).

Thanks to his mother, he inherited Kilkenny and other lands in Ireland. In 1252, he came to Tewkesbury to spend Easter but after a very active military life he was laid to rest at Tewkesbury and buried on 28th July 1262, it is writ with great solemnity in the presence of two bishops and eight abbots in the presbytery at his father's right hand. Richard's own arms were: Or, three chevronels gules.

Gilbert de Clare,
3rd Earl of Gloucester
(born 2nd September 1243 Christchurch, Hampshire died 7th December 1295)
known as 'Red' Gilbert due to his bright red hair. He built Caerffili (Caerphilly) Castle in Morgannwg (Glamorgan). He married Joan of Acre, daughter of Edward I. In 1264 fighting with Prince Edward Longshanks (later to become Edward I) they took possession of Gloucester and Bristol and were declared rebels in their own land! Red took action by destroying the bridge over the Severn and ships at Bristol to prevent Simon de Montfort escaping. He died at Monmouth Castle and was buried at Tewkesbury on the left hand side of his grandfather, Gilbert.

Gilbert de Clare,
4th Earl of Gloucester from 1295
(born 1291 died 24th June 1314) was the grandson of Edward I and his first wife, Eleanor of Castile but died young whilst fighting the Scots. He had no heirs and so the title became extinct again.

Ralph de Monthermer, Earl of Gloucester from 1299 *(died 1325)*

acquired earldoms through his marriage to Gilbert the Red's widow Joan of Acre (who was also daughter of no-nonsense Edward I). Edward was furious about this lowly second marriage as he had other ideas and was busy playing matchmaker by arranging her marriage to an Italian noble.

Despite Ralph being held prisoner at Bannockburn on behalf of Edward's wars, he was thrown in prison again, this time by a frustrated father-in-law, and Joan had to plead for his release. According to the St Albans chronicler, she told her father, 'No one sees anything wrong if a great earl marries a poor and lowly woman. Why should there be anything wrong if a countess marries a young and promising man?' Her father relented, released Monthermer from gaol in August 1297, and allowed him to hold the title of Earl of Gloucester during Joan's lifetime. He lost his titles on her death in 1307.

Hugh Audley, 1st Earl of Gloucester from 1337

(born 1289 in Stretton Audley, Oxfordshire, died on 10th November 1347 in France) Hugh married Margaret de Clare on 28th April 1317 in Windsor, Berkshire. Margaret was born in 1293 in Gloucestershire and as daughter of Sir Gilbert 'The Red' de Clare and Joan of Acre she carried the title of Earl of Gloucester. Margaret was the first wife of Piers Gaveston, Edward II's intimate favourite. In his lifetime Hugh became Ambassador to France in 1341; his wife died on 13th April 1342 in France.

Thomas Le Despencer, 1st Earl of Gloucester from 1397 degraded 1399 *(born 1373 died 1400)*, supported

Richard II and was awarded the Gloucester earldom in the king's fight against Thomas of Woodstock. However, he supported Henry Bolingbroke's drive to become Henry IV and was to be deprived of the earldom for his part in Woodstock's death. What goes around . . . he was finally dishonoured and beheaded at Bristol when he took part in a rebellion to restore Richard II.

Some Other Noble Gloucesters

Robert of Gloucester 1260–1300, English Chronicler

Possibly a monk of Gloucester, he was a chronicler during his lifetime. More than one person may have written the chronicle, which covers the period from the legendary Brut to 1270, for the two sections vary. It is important however for the study of words at the time and an historical source for the Barons' War in the reign of Henry III.

Miles or Fitzmiles of Gloucester

Milo or Miles FitzWalter known as Miles of Gloucester was a prominent landowner from the Gloucestershire area, whose father held the offices of both sheriff and justice for the county. Miles died in a hunting accident on the Christmas Eve of 1143. He married Sybil de Neufmarché in 1121 and they had eight children. Miles was particularly busy during the 'Caedfael' period of history when the cousins Stephen and Matilda fought for succession. So instrumental was he in many and varied aspects of Gloucester life he founded Llanthony Secunda Priory as refuge for the monks from Monmouthshire.

Miles Smith Bishop of Gloucester

Miles Smith was born in Hereford in 1554; in 1612 he was appointed Bishop of Gloucester and he was buried in the cathedral at the age of 70. His contemporaries paid him the tribute of 'proved at length an incomparable theologist', and he was known for his brilliance in Biblical languages. This austere Calvinist graduated through Oxford University, became resident canon of Hereford Cathedral and was awarded his Doctor of Divinity in 1594. Miles was responsible for the translation of the Old Testament for the King James Version of the Bible and hand in glove with the Bishop of Winchester was in charge of the final proofs before it went to the printers. It is his Preface which marries up with the Authorised Version.

Shakespeare

Edmund Glouster is one of the players in King Lear. He is the bastard son of the Earl of Gloucester. Edmund plots against his half-brother Edgar as well as his father, and various other members of the cast, and becomes involved in a love triangle with Goneril and Regan and is ambitious, scheming and duplicitous.

Dukes of Gloucester pop up in various plays by the bard, impressing the import of this title both in history and in Shakespeare's eyes and writings.

" before entering the great
cathedral doors cast your
eyes up to the gargoyles "

Gloucester Cathedral

If you want to read cheesy lines like the Jewel of Gloucester or Gloucester's treasure, or jargon about architecture and all that jazz, then you're reading the wrong book.

I came to Gloucester Cathedral many years ago essentially for one reason: to worship. When you enter remember this marvel was built over the original wooden Anglo-Saxon abbey to glorify the new religion that was sweeping these lands: Christianity. For all the spiritual awe this glorious place can inspire, everything, even a garden folly, has its reason for being and St Peter's Abbey-cum-Gloucester Cathedral was no exception.

Before entering the great cathedral doors cast your eyes up to the gargoyles. The word 'gargoyle' shares a root with the words 'gargle' and 'gurgle'; they all come from *'gargouille'*, a Norman French word for 'throat'. A gargoyle does precisely that; gulps down and spews out excess waters from the guttering along the roof. The brilliant mason, Pascal Mychalysin, has sculpted brand new creatures, and as I write this book has already created some fascinating faces that wouldn't be out of place in a Hammer House of Horror flick or a Cumbrian gurning competition.

It is wonderful to know that we have craftsmen around in the 21st century to carry on a tradition that began when ace designer and architect, Serlo, was sent for by William I (the Conqueror or Bastard) from Mont St Michel in Normandy to create a permanent stone building: work began on this hallowed spot on 29th June 1089. The abbey was consecrated on 15th July 1100. There's a saying 'use it or lose it' and thank heavens (quite literally) to the cathedral powers-that-be in this new millennium who are not just preserving but creating carvings that combine ancient and modern so beautifully. We nearly lost a religious building on this site when Osric's abbey burned down in 1088 and again when Henry VIII fought the Pope. Let us make sure we keep this cathedral in constant use so there is never a chance we will ever come close to losing it again.

Enter in. Once inside God's house, whisper a little prayer or light a candle, do what people have done for centuries. It takes a mason many hours to carve a gargoyle but it takes a much shorter time to carry on this compassionate and humbling ritual of worship.

daughter of the King of France, was intent on taking power, and let's not rule out a spot of revenge too. She had a very well-connected lover, Roger Mortimer, 1st Earl of March, all of which contributed to Edward's eventual downfall and death. It is worth considering his murder, which is reputed to have been a poker thrust up where the sun don't shine, is just a myth for historians are now pretty confident that this was a ghastly rumour set about by the Tudors who were no friends of the Plantagenets. It is probable Edward was suffocated in Berkeley Castle not far from Gloucester. Some say he never died there at all but escaped to Corfe Castle in Dorset where he was holed up and then murdered, or disguised as a hermit he made good to the continent and settled in Milan in Lombardy (now northern Italy) where he lived out the rest of his life.

Which leads to the question, whose bones are in the tomb if these tales are right? I was assured during my visit that the remains within are those of Edward II. Besides, in medieval times, kings were embalmed which meant all kinds of intimate preparations were carried out before burial. Not easy to fake. Edward was laid in a coffin of lead which was then placed in one of wood. This was then handed over to the Abbot of St Peter's Abbey (which was to become Gloucester Cathedral in due course) and the king was laid to rest where you are now.

His son, Edward III, transformed the tomb into a place for pilgrims by creating a candlelit spectacle, burnishing it with gold and brilliant colours that would wow the visitors – like a pop icon or movie star; then, the royals, much like now were the celebrity of the age.

Almost opposite to Edward in the South Ambulatory is the tomb of Robert of Normandy with his strangely handsome but physically contorted effigy carved from Irish

There is much to see so I am only going to proffer you my favourites, so you can share in them and along the way discover your own.

Hot foot it round to the North Ambulatory. Edward II's tomb is incredible. Not only because it has been there since 1327 (it was his son, Edward III, who had the pinnacled canopy put in the place with a tomb of alabaster and Purbeck marble) but because of the controversial life of this Plantagenet king, and the fact that he is one of few sovereigns buried outside of Westminster – even though the Plantagenets made more of a habit of it than most.

This unfortunate monarch born between two powerful macho men, Edward I and Edward III, was a bisexual who had his male favourites – Piers Gaveston and Hugh le Despenser. In this dynastic drama the woman scorned, his wife Queen Isabella,

bog oak. As the eldest son of William I – who loved Gloucester – Robert had an unfulfilled life being beaten to the English throne by his brother who became Henry I, and in 1106 imprisoned by his bro; in all he spent 28 years captive in Cardiff Castle. Robert was interred in the abbey around 900 years ago yet looking at him it seems he will never be at rest, always at the ready to attack or defend, with hand on sword.

Head back to near Edward II's tomb and find Osric's. He may be little known but this Anglo-Saxon royal is more important than his lack of fame would suggest. Osric was the ruler of the local tribe, the Hwicce, a lesser kingdom under the sway of either Wessex or Mercia, with Mercia eventually winning the tussle. Apart from being the Hwicce king or prince he became viceroy to King Ethelred of Mercia too. Although the tomb has been given a Tudor makeover, his life and times were crucially important to the cathedral as it was he who first brought Christianity to the Gloucester area. Osric is claimed as the founder of two monastic houses, Bath Abbey and in AD 679 (some say 681) Gloucester's St Peter's Abbey. That is why he clasps the abbey's successor, a mini Gloucester Cathedral, to his bosom – Tudor style of course. In 1022 the abbey was reformed under the Benedictine order.

It was having the three royal tombs here, all ancestors of Henry VIII, that saved the building. When Henry was involved in a battle of wills with the Pope in Rome he dissolved the monasteries to show who was boss in England and Wales. Gloucester Cathedral was saved as the egotistical and paranoid king did not want the building that housed 'his ancestor's bodies' to be destroyed; after all he had declared himself Defender of the Faith so his word was now religious law. Cleverly he or someone close suggested that as the Diocese of Worcester (of which Gloucester was then a part) was so huge, the southern part be carved out, St Peter's Abbey given the prestige of cathedral status and the new Diocese of Gloucester created – job done, building saved and we can enjoy it today.

Look to the stained glass windows now: the great east window, this is one of the most stunning medieval windows in any building dating back to the time of the mid 1300s. The only time it has been in jeopardy was in World War II when each pane was stored in the crypt to keep it safe from bombing. However the dampness down below over a period of six years destroyed the numbers of each pane written on paper,

leaving a complicated jigsaw to be pieced together – some say that only one mistake was made when it was returned after the war. Can you spot it? What was it? Who can say? Is there one or just a ruse to keep you looking and guessing!

On 28th October 1216 Henry III was crowned in the cathedral at the age of 9 years old. Head back to the South Aisle near where you came in, look up to see the king in his glory being crowned with – what is it? Because the ceremony was staged in a frenzied hurry due to political forces closing in on him, plus the small thing that King John had lost the crown jewels in the wastes of The Wash (oh yes he did!) his politically active mum, Isabella of Angoulême, produced a piece of her jewellery (a bracelet or torque) and he was crowned – short notice and not exactly a diadem, but it did the trick. Henry was king.

Across from Henry by the steps at the North Transept is a marble plaque commemorating the man who wrote the music for the American National Anthem. John Stafford Smith was born in 1750 and christened in Gloucester Cathedral. After his education at the Cathedral School he was a choir boy at the Chapel Royal in London. He studied under his dad, Martin Smith, who was organist at the cathedral for 42 years, but soon gained a reputation of his own and was given membership of the select Anacreontic Society. Members have included J.S. Bach and Henry Purcell.

In 1780 he composed the music for the society's club song. It was entitled 'To Anacreon in Heaven'. Inspired by the hedonistic lifestyle of the 5th/6th century classical Greek poet Anacreon it celebrated the pleasures of wine and love and was sung at the Crown and Anchor Tavern in the Strand, London where they held their meetings. The club song became popular both in Britain and America for probably all the wrong reasons! In 1814 Francis Scott Key wrote the words to what became officially in 1931 one of the most famous national anthems in the world. I bet when John Stafford Smith died in 1836 he never thought he would have made the top ten of the international hit parade.

Time for a break? Pop into the cathedral shop, I so enjoy a wander choosing wee gifties. Sorry folks I know some people think souvenir shops are full of dust collectors but they are great places to buy a token that records the memory of a visit that might never be made by me or you again AND you are making a financial contribution to the cathedral's upkeep. Good for all.

IN MEMORY OF
JOHN STAFFORD SMITH
1750-1836 who, born in this city, son of Martin Smith organist of the Cathedral 1743-1782, was a composer of distinction, a well-known musical antiquary, and organist of the Chapel Royal London. He will long be remembered as composer of the tune of the National Anthem of the United States of America

Out to the coffee shop for a cuppa with a display of tasty home-made cakes and other fancies. Refreshed? Now prepare to be wowed. Take the route to the toilets, following the signpost to the cloisters – look up and around, isn't this something?

Sit awhile on a bench and drift back to how the monks would have lived and in wonderment at how ordinary men could have created such a work of art way back in the 14th century.

The coffee shop is the bottom floor of the Parliament Room – above it is the room where Gloucester hosted Richard II's parliament in 1378.

Gloucester became the administrative capital of England and Wales three times in its history. Now this room that once echoed to kings and nobles houses all kinds of functions from conventions to social gatherings.

There is much, much more to see in the cathedral than I have described but these are the attractions that appeal to me, and I am sure there is even more that will appeal to you personally.

For more information go to the website: *www.gloucestercathedral.org.uk*

“ if you have a fertile imagination then you will
be able to feel the ghosts of an age gone by ”

St Oswald's Priory

. . . or the Minster of St Oswald. The almost insignificant ruins belie a holy place of great past importance and one of my most favourite places in the city.

If you have a fertile imagination then you will be able to feel the ghosts of an age gone by. St Oswald's Priory was founded by that great Saxon husband-and-wife double-act, the Lord of Mercia, Aethelred II, and his wife, Aethelflaed, daughter of King Alfred. Aethelred was subject to Alfred, who was his overlord.

Aethelflaed, known as the Lady of the Mercians, was a combination of Boudicca, Queen Elizabeth I and Margaret Thatcher, so you get the idea that she had the kind of grit needed for a woman to survive in a strictly male and very savage world. She had taken control of the Kingdom of Mercia when her husband was laid low in his later years as a result of a debilitating illness that led to his death in 911; after then Aethelflaed took over the royal reins completely. The Kingdom of Mercia was subject to Alfred and Wessex during all this period so this merely strengthened the union between two of the greatest Saxon kingdoms. In 890 or thereabouts, the foundations for the priory were laid, perhaps even to evoke divine help to aid Aethelred's recovery: he could have been ill for two years or more before the cornerstones were grounded.

Gloucester had already been earmarked by Lady Aethelflaed for a major renovation as one of the defensive boroughs network that Alfred had instituted throughout his lands, and his daughter, a real chip off the old block, carried on his work. The city was destined for a major facelift and total rebuild bristling with fortifications to fend off attacks from the Vikings who would sail up the River Severn from Brittany or Danes who were already encroaching into other parts of Mercia. Gloucester was one of a number of key places that would make a fine catch for any marauding army. Aethelflaed was the making of modern Gloucester, for example today's road layout is due not so much to the Romans as this feisty lady.

There were few sacred buildings of such grandeur built during this part of the Saxon period probably due to all hands being on deck fighting the invaders, so there was little time to erect expensive churches. Originally, the priory church was dedicated to St Peter, and mainly constructed from stones used by the Romans to create Glevum. It is said masonry from a Roman temple was used in its building; there were reasons for this, by utilising pagan stones in a Christian holy place it eradicated any bad heathen vibes. Most constructions in Saxon times were made of wood so they had to be pretty special to warrant such expensive materials; it was the Normans who came with their stones and masons and set a more solid trend.

It may be hard to believe now when you walk around the site, with a main road on one side and houses the other that you are standing on a Christian cemetery once complete with beautifully carved crosses. It was so ornate that it was probably reserved for Mercian nobles or royalty especially as Kingsholm palace was so near. It was also described as a Minster church, often known as the last of the Minsters.

The first church was erected in the 890s, nothing too special although there was a continental influence to its structure. But it was in 909 when the Mercians were really coming into their own, thanks to the fighting Lady Aethelflaed and her husband, that they obtained relics of the 7th century kingly saint, Oswald of Northumbria – and they knew that their special Gloucester church was the perfect place to keep them safe.

King St Oswald had been laid to rest in Lincolnshire, in Bardney Abbey to be exact, which had been destroyed by Viking invaders. King Edward the Elder of Wessex – another of Alfred's brood and Aethelflaed's brother – made safe with the torso (the other parts of the body were taken to other places all over the country) after his audacious attack on Viking territory.

The remains were brought to Gloucester with great pious majesty and ceremony and interred in the new royal priory church. As befits the remains of a saint and king an ornate crypt had been prepared and carvings, paintings and wall hangings added to increase the prestige of this new Saxon shrine. It was at this point St Peter made way for St Oswald in the dedication stakes as Aethelflaed and Aethelred had by now chosen to be buried in the eastern crypt alongside their very own patron saint.

Like Gloucester Cathedral centuries later for Edward II, pilgrims travelled to St Oswald's for word had gone out about this amazing new attraction and it soon became a national shrine. Gifts from the worshippers enabled the priory to flourish with both lands and treasures, although it was never a rich set-up and at one time was in debt to local Jews.

The Minster became the centre of a large parish and was decreed a Royal Free Chapel (not under the powers of the bishops) and maintained a chapel at Kingsholm Palace. In the 10th century the building was extended with the addition of

a tower. The canons produced their own bells as a bell-pit was excavated on this exact site by the Gloucester Archaeological Society; a mould was discovered with the Greek letters Alpha and Omega, the beginning and the end, which was, of course, the sign for God.

In 1070, the priory was given to the care of the Archbishop of York; this arrangement lasted until 1536, although Edward I created a break in the continuity due to a dispute between three ecclesiastics.

When William I came to Gloucester about two years after having taken his place in English history the place was already in decline. The Archbishop of York reformed the priory in 1153 and Augustinian monks were invited to take the place of the secular monks. St Peter's Abbey (to become Gloucester Cathedral) had little power when St Oswald's Priory was at its height but now the priory was on the wane and the abbey, thanks to William I and Serlo, was on the rise.

Thankfully, the priory survived Henry VIII's Dissolution of the Monasteries in the 1530s, as did St Peter's Abbey which became Gloucester Cathedral. In 1548 the arches of the north aisle were blocked up and it became the popular parish church of St Catherine.

Throughout the centuries royals had built it, enlarged it, saved it and now they were the ones to destroy it as a result of King Charles I's Royalist cannon fire during the Siege of Gloucester and by 1653 much of it was demolished. The stone was used by the city council in 1655 to build a new market house in Eastgate Street.

Knowing all this history, give yourself a treat and flex your mental muscle. The standing remains are the north wall of Aethelflaed's original building, one large round-headed arch is Saxon, the others are of the 12th and 13th centuries. It is likely that the Lady herself is buried in the back garden of the house nearest the ruins; with your back to the main ring road, look to your left and the garden nearest to you could harbour Gloucester's top lady, and of course where's her husband Aethelred's body and what became of the relics?

To add to the conundrum head for the Gloucester City Museum & Art Gallery where a beautifully carved grave cover can be seen that must have belonged to a very important or noble person, could it be theirs? If that doesn't add spice to your imagination it's hard to imagine what would!

What didn't help the image of the priory was the bitter argument over its ownership between the Archbishops of York and Canterbury and Bishop of Worcester. This resulted in a dog in a manger edict by the Bishop of Worcester who when he couldn't get his own way excommunicated the canons of St Oswald's and even forbade the citizens of Gloucester from doing any business with them. King Edward I intervened and came to its rescue. He reasserted the Royal Free Chapel status it had gained in Saxon times and declared the priory exempt from the bishops and lifted Worcester's ban.

Llanthony Priory

Llanthony Secunda Priory to give its full name is now nothing more than the beautiful and evocative remains of a medieval priory of Augustinian canons.

Today it is still known as Secunda to separate it from the original Llanthony Priory Prima in Monmouthshire where the first canons came over from.

Prima was seized in 1136 by the Welsh (British) rebels during the civil war between Stephen and Matilda. Llanthony Secunda was founded in the same year to house the fugitive prior and around two dozen canons. Miles of Gloucester supplied the land, which was attached to his own Gloucester Castle. His descendants, the Bohuns, were the hereditary Constables of England, and were buried for ten generations in the priory church and chapter house. Although many may now be in a watery grave after the building of the canal to Sharpness.

Miles was very active in this civil war of succession, first with Stephen and then against him aligning with his cousin the Empress Matilda, often called Maud.

By 1150 the new priory had stately buildings with glorious gardens and vineyards. Come the peace the Prima site was restored after 1154 but the priors remained in Gloucester and accordingly Secunda prospered. The two communities separated in 1205 until 1481.

Royal patronage in the form of Henry III, crowned at Gloucester, came in 1241 when he arrived with his court to discuss and enact affairs of state at Secunda. The Dowager Queen Eleanor living in Gloucester Castle in 1277 was given permission to walk in the prior's garden. King Edward II was imprisoned here on the way to meet his doom at Berkeley Castle.

In 1301 the church was gutted by fire. The west front was rebuilt but most of the fabric surviving above ground today dates from the end of the 15th century when the then prior, Henry Deane, reconstructed both church and precinct, including the outer gatehouse. The coats of arms of many benefactors of the priory are of King Henry VII; the Bohun family, supporters of the priory for 200 years; and Henry Deane the Prior of Secunda and Bishop of Bangor, Caernarfonshire.

In 1349 an unwelcome guest, the Black Death, took the souls of 19 of the 30 canons. During Richard II's Parliament in Gloucester 1378 it was the scene of the gallows for one of Simon de Montfort's stable lads found guilty of murder. The Duke of Buckingham was stationed here in 1381 with 200 men ready to quell unrest in the city. The two priories united again in 1481 when Llanthony Secunda bought out its mother church.

By this time Llanthony Secunda was the richest Augustinian house in England, noted for its opulent entertaining and hospitality. It welcomed the court of Henry VII in 1500 and 1501 it is said for medicinal reasons. The Tudor king raised the prior to become Archbishop of Canterbury. The priory was dissolved in 1538 by Henry VII's son, Henry VIII, and in 1540 much of the site was sold.

Three generations of the Porter family used the priory as their country house until 1632. During the Civil War Llanthony suffered damage from both sides, especially in the 1643 Siege of Gloucester when Llanthony served as a base for the besieging Royalists.

The town clerk ordered the demolition of the priory tower to prevent it becoming a viewfinder for marksmen. After all the bombarding the priory was a shadow of its former self.

Rather than rebuild the historic priory, it was eventually included in the adjoining parish of Hempsted which was upgraded as a result of having such an illustrious ward. This was also the end of Llanthony House as a home and after 1670 the timber-studded range was converted into a farmhouse.

In the mid-19th century the site was re-designed to create Llanthony Abbey Farm. The importance of the, to me, beautiful remains of the priory was officially recognised in 1949 when the site was protected as a Scheduled Ancient Monument. In 1974 British Railways sold it to Gloucester City Council.

The church wasn't always in the holy business for in 1643 it was a prison for 1500 soldiers captured at Highnam by the Parliamentarian Governor of Gloucester Garrison, Edward Massey. Due to the food shortage the men were held for ten days fed on nothing but vegetable leftovers; they were then released with a promise not to fight against Parliament again. In 1646 the church was again a prison, this time for prisoners from Stow on the Wold.

St Mary De Lode Church

The word Lode (or Lád) is derived from Anglo-Saxon meaning a water way or water course particularly through marshy or fenny ground; in the British language Lod interprets as a wet place or swamp. At one time there was a branch of the river to the west of the church which is long gone, so it is likely there was a guide or ferry across what was obviously treacherous terrain.

The church is almost surely the city of Gloucester's oldest parish church (some say the oldest Christian place in Britain even) and according to local legend it was the burial place of King Lucius of Britain who in the 2nd century created a bishopric in Gloucester. A church of some sorts was built on the site of a 5th-century Roman temple. According to that master of news of the times, the Venerable Bede, Lucius was converted to Christianity in AD 105. In addition Robert of Gloucester's Chronicle states that the British king died in Gloucester four years after his conversion.

Between the cathedral and St Mary de Lode Church, Bishop Hooper was martyred for his Protestant face refusing to convert to Catholicism during Mary I's turbulent Tudor reign. His statue stands aloof between cathedral and church on the spot that was too hot for him to survive in 1555.

St Mary de Crypt and the Three Friaries

Right in the heart of the city many generations of Gloucestrians have worshipped at a church here since 1140 and that's a conservative estimate.

The church was placed under the welfare of Llanthony Secunda Priory in 1241, when this prosperous priory began a massive rebuilding programme on St Mary's which peaked in the late 1300s. The crypt was used as a charnel house in the medieval period storing bones of the deceased.

Around 1576 it was turned into an Elizabethan pub until the British Civil War when it became a wood shed and explosive store for Parliament and the Gloucester Garrison. Take a look at the sundial outside which has its own wee bit of history with the impact of a shot from the Royalist gunners clearly visible. I personally like the iron-mace used by the Mayor during George II's reign, iron being symbolic and representative of a part of Gloucester's prosperity. But for me the real highlight is the glorious wall painting fully revealed in 1982. Dated *circa* 1520s the *Adoration of the Magi* is from the

Flemish school and as was the done thing in those days the little figure waving at you is the artist himself!

You will find monuments to one and all including brasses to John and Joan Cooke, founders of the Crypt Grammar School in 1539. The school relocated in 1861 to Barton Street and Greyfriars and in 1943/4 to its current site.

Greyfriars

The house of the Franciscan Grey Friars of Gloucester, near the South Gate of the town, was founded about 1231 on land donated by Thomas I of Berkeley. King Henry III, a total Gloucesterphile and devout Christian, granted oak and other building timbers from his royal Forest of Dean and elsewhere. It was one of three Gloucester monasteries supported by Henry III whose coronation was at Gloucester Cathedral. Agnellus of Pisa guided the friars in their work. They at first accepted only a small plot of land but soon after in 1239 they needed more and, by the persuasion of his wife, Thomas of Berkeley gave more. In 1246 Henry III allowed them to hold schools of theology in a turret of the town wall and by 1277 there were 24 friars and up to 40 by 1284, the numbers increasing so much that in 1285 the friars needed even more land.

A holy war broke out when they came into conflict with the Benedictines of St Peter's Abbey (Gloucester Cathedral) who stole a corpse destined for burial in Greyfriars; in those days money was involved which obviously ended up in the Benedictine coffers. In the middle of the fourteenth century they were battling again, this time when the friars claimed the right to the water coming from a spring at Breresclyft, Robinswood Hill. This time they won thanks to none other than Edward III; the Black Prince called in their favour on a visit to Gloucester in 1357. Come 1518 the Berkeley family again showed their patronage by helping to rebuild the priory.

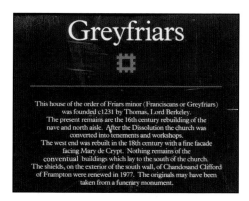

This house of the order of Friars minor (Franciscans or Greyfriars) was founded c1231 by Thomas, Lord Berkeley. The present remains are the 16th century rebuilding of the nave and north aisle. After the Dissolution the church was converted into tenements and workshops. The west end was rebuilt in the 18th century with a fine facade facing Mary de Crypt. Nothing remains of the conventual buildings which lay to the south of the church. The shields, on the exterior of the south wall, of Chandos and Clifford of Frampton were renewed in 1977. The originals may have been taken from a funerary monument.

In 1538 at the time of Dissolution of the monasteries Richard Ingworth reported to Henry VIII's Lord Privy Seal, Thomas Cromwell, in charge of the destruction of the monasteries, that Greyfriars was 'a goodly house, much of it new builded'. It obviously wasn't to save the friary for worship but to see how much it would make on the property market for the royal exchequer. Many of the Grey Friars had already packed up and left for the continent after the Act of Supremacy in 1534, leaving just five to bear the consequences of closure in 1538.

Following their departure the church – with its abundant water supply – became a brewery. During the Siege of Gloucester it was damaged by Royalist cannon fire and by 1721 the chancels and cloisters were gone.

It was converted into residences, an apothecary's lab, and at one point it was lodgings for sailors. In its final days it was a liquor store before, thankfully, being declared a monument in the 1960s.

Greyfriars House

In 1810 Greyfriars House – now a library – was built into one end. It was built on an existing building that belonged to Sir John Powell MP for Gloucester in 1685. His story as a judge is one of open-mindedness and fairness; when a wretched so-called witch Jane Wenman was accused of flying, he said she was innocent as there was no law that he knew of against flying! When he died in 1713 he was given a place of honour in Gloucester Cathedral – on his epitaph it is worth noting a tribute given by John Powell who knew Sir John: 'He was the merriest old gentleman I ever saw, spoke pleasing things and chuckled till he cried' – my kind of guy!

Whitefriars

The house of the White or Carmelite Friars of Gloucester outside the North Gate had its origin about 1268 and was founded with the help of Queen Eleanor, King Henry's wife, Sir Thomas Giffard, and Thomas of Berkeley. We also know that that goodly king, Henry III, supplied the timbers as he did for the other Gloucester religious houses. In 1337 the number of friars was thirty-one and in 1343 Edward III allowed them to acquire a few acres of land from Thomas of Berkeley. In 1347, by an agreement with the prior and brethren of St Bartholomew's hospital, they obtained water running through a leaden pipe from 'Gosewhytewell' spring. On 25th July, 1538, at the Dissolution, Thomas Cromwell, the architect of Henry VIII's tyranny, was told that the White Friars were 'ready to surrender'. Amen.

Blackfriars

The house of the Black Friars of Gloucester was founded about 1239 just over 20 years after the order had been founded and St Dominic came on a mission to these islands in 1221, only four years after the Dominicans were formed. It is probable that Stephen, Lord of Harnhill, gave the site to the religious house, built on land on the bailey of William I's (the Conqueror's) castle; King Henry III got stuck in with his gifts of timber yet again. It took over twenty-five years to build and in 1246 King Henry dipped into his pocket giving 41 marks for extra land, a churchyard, and making a direct road connecting the friary to Gloucester's main street.

A seal of the 13th century shows one bald-headed and bearded man in flowing garments, holding a book and a reversed sword by the point, probably St Paul; the other tonsured, in the habit of the Friars Preachers, holding a long cross and a book; in base the half figure of a prior at prayer.

In the first half of the 14th century the number of friars varied from thirty to forty. They were primarily preachers and teachers as well as confessors to the rich and powerful. Evidence of their community practice was dug up in 1991 with many skeletons of women and children, including that of a young woman with hereditary syphilis being excavated from the cemetery. The young woman left people scratching their heads as the disease was said to have come to Britain around 80 years after! It is thought there are another couple of thousand more bodies buried in the friary's medieval precinct.

It is probable that, as at Bristol and elsewhere, many of the Gloucester Black Friars left these shores on the Act of Supremacy in 1534 and 1535 and the few who remained were in abject poverty, and had sold the greater part of their goods, even their chalices made of precious metal had been changed to tin and copper.

On 25th July, 1538, Richard Ingworth sent back his report to Thomas Cromwell that the Black Friars were ready to give in and give up.

In 1539 the priory was purchased by Sir Thomas Bell. He put it to good use and in a way carried on the Dominicans' work by employing about a tenth of the city's population making knitted caps, as well as living there with his family. By the 1930s the glorious scriptorium was a mineral water bottling factory, part of the west range a pub.

Times change and now the priory with its magnificent timbered roof is the most complete survival of a medieval Dominican priory in Britain. The original medieval cloister, completed in 1239, includes my personal favourite, the scriptorium, where the monks worked over 750 years ago. This is believed to be Britain's oldest surviving library building. When I toured the place I was in awe. I can't remember seeing anything like it in my well travelled life. You can still see and touch the heavy iron rings buried in the walls where the precious books were security-attached. You can see, feel and even hear the past in this amazing place filled with amazing grace.

Kingsholm

The chances are you're more likely to hear Kingsholm bandied around in pursuit of the game of rugby rather than in its original role as a most important Saxon royal palace.

Gloucester RUFC, one of the leading clubs in the sport, play at a ground called Kingsholm; it is likely where the original royal palace lay.

It was in the late AD 40s–early AD 50s that the Romans came to visit and chose a spot near the lowest possible crossing of the River Severn and stayed by building a fortress. Around 20 years later the centre was moved because it was on the Severn flood plain and almost certainly became waterlogged, so a new fortress was built on higher ground, on the site of the current city centre, although some schools of thought suggest the fort was built just north of Gloucester at Kingsholm in the 60s AD and was abandoned after just a decade.

In the 5th century, to the west of the present Kingsholm Road, the usefulness of the place may have survived at the hub of a Roman farming estate.

Perhaps it was owned by a local nobleman, or possibly an Ostrogoth mercenary who in 1972 was discovered at Kingsholm Close buried inside a re-used Roman stone mausoleum. The Ostrogoths came from an area now occupied by modern day Italy, Slovenia, Hungary and Croatia.

The importance of Kingsholm did not end with the collapse of the Roman Empire.

Gloucester's number one fan during Saxon times was Aethelflaed, Lady of the Mercians; a warrior queen, daughter of King Alfred and very much in the mode of Boudicca. We know that she and her husband, Aethelred II, built St Oswald's Priory just down the road and kept a Royal Free Chapel, linked to the priory, at Kingsholm which by the 9th century was a Saxon Royal Palace. By 896 a Mercian council met in or near the town undoubtedly at Kingsholm.

Apart from Aethelflaed and consort it was used by Danish King Cnut and King Edward the Confessor.

We know for dead cert that Kingsholm Palace did exist as we have proof positive in Saxon documents. Certainly parts of 10th/11th-century buildings have been excavated immediately north of Kingsholm Close, including a large timber-framed hall. I visited this site: there is a large square piece of rough grass which contained probably only a small part of the actual palace building, and as the Saxons built in wood it is probably this hall that was the main palace building. A hoard of early 11th-century coins have also been found, so big that it was unlikely to belong to a single person unless they were a rich royal, but it is thought they may be taxes from a region of which Kingsholm was the civic centre. A visit to Gloucester City Museum & Art Gallery will reveal an impressive array of coins that have been found in and around the city.

Norman monarchs have stayed here, with William the Conqueror using the Palace as his home in his usual Christmas tradition. He spent the festivities every year at Gloucester and to hold Witan (Parliament).

The one of 1085 could well have been centred on Kingsholm and it is debatable if it was here he gave the order for the Domesday Book to be compiled; popular thought is the Chapter House at St Peter's Abbey. Wherever, the palace makes its own appearance in the inventory with the king's hall and chamber being mentioned. 1086 was the last time he held court in Gloucester.

Don't think of Kingsholm as being just one building stuck out on its own, for the whole palace area needed to be vast as it had to regularly house the king and his enormous national retinue.

When Henry III was crowned in the Cathedral (then still St Peter's Abbey) the young prince (he was just 9 years old) started his journey to kingship appropriately enough from Kingsholm on 28th October 1216.

Kingsholm's importance declined when the Normans built their massive castle where the prison is now, possibly around the 1120s.

Silver penny of Aethelred II, struck in Gloucester by his moneyer Leofsige, AD 997–1003

" the River Severn or Afon Hafren
    at 219 miles is Britain's longest "

River Severn/Afon Hafren

It doesn't take a geographical genius to know that any city or town of prestige, success and importance has a river running through it.

A place requires not only a good water supply but also a highway to get in and out of the home base and onto the high seas. In the days before good roads it was the river that was at the heart of positive communications. Whether for supplies, invasion, recreation or trade a river is a must. And if you're going to have a river then the Severn or Hafren is about as good as you can get. The River Severn or Afon Hafren at 219 miles is Britain's longest; it rises on Plynlimon/Pumlumon – the Five Beacons – on the borders of Cardiganshire and Montgomeryshire in the Cambrian Mountains.

For Gloucester the River Severn has proven to be something that little bit more special. As an inland port it is probably more in-land than any other in the country and is at the lowest point on the river where it is bridgeable. The tidal surge (which has become a legend and a local phenomenon known as the Bore) rushes up as far as the city itself, good for fish and great for surfers.

Gloucester's earliest origins suggest there was some kind of British habitation around this part of the Severn probably to the north of where the main city evolved and developed. It is also more than likely that natural activity in or on the river gave Gloucester its name of the bright shiny place perhaps through light dancing on the water or fish shining like silver within its ripples.

The Romans recognised its worth as being ideal for incursions into the British camps and strongholds in what we now call Wales or Cymru. The Anglo-Saxons certainly knew Gloucester was the perfect place to build a royal palace and King Alfred's daughter, Aethelflaed, favoured the city creating holy sites, increasing the royal connection and transforming it into an important fortified borough, which included updating the inner city road network, and making it a prime HQ in her fight against the Danes and as an important centre for the powerful Kingdom of the Mercians.

The Normans too enjoyed the city with William I taking it easy over many Christmases there, and the Plantagenets left one of their monarchs, Edward II, in situ for ever more in the cathedral, which added to Gloucester's halo as angel of the Severn. Richard III gave the city the same civic powers as London and to this day much of the local government of Gloucester is based on his expansive and influential charter.

Elizabeth I blessed Gloucester with port status – which meant that slippery traders and merchants who bypassed Bristol and sailed straight up the Severn to save on import/export duties got a rude awakening from 1580 when the city could levy its own taxes on shipping, much to Bristol's chagrin.

By the time of the Stuarts leading up to Cromwell's wars and the Siege of Gloucester, the river proved, yet again, how important it was as a base for transport into the West, Midlands, North and South West. The power of the Severn has never waned.

From the Hanoverians onwards Gloucester may have lost its lustre as a royal base but the name continued to live on either in warships, fighter planes, dukedoms or Beatrix Potter fairy tales with one HMS *Gloucester* even paying a ceremonial visit to the Docks in 1911 before war broke out.

The Severn Bore (almost as famous as the Severn Bridge!) is one of those bizarre things that you can imagine in the darker ages of history the locals must have wondered what on earth was going on. Perhaps Noah and his flood sprang to their gullible minds or the Gods were angry and sending a tsunami to show that they were angry: worse still was it the end of the world? When the science of navigation and tides discovered the reasons were more elemental than divine spirits who were unhappy and seeking retribution, a little bit of mystique was taken out of the Bore. I am grateful to Russell Higgins' excellent page on the Severn Bore; he has a website with timetables of when it can be seen so you can plan your trip around what you find out on *www.severn-bore.co.uk/*

But what is the Severn Bore? Basically it is a large surge wave that rushes up the estuary of the River Severn.

The river estuary has to be the right shape and the tidal conditions such that the wave is able to form. The Severn Bore is large by world standards but by far the biggest is the Ch'ient'ang'kian (Hang-chou-fe) in China. It is heard advancing at a range of 14 miles; you can even hear the Severn Bore some miles off.

Look at a map of Wales and the West of England to see the loop de loop around the Severn estuary. The water is funnelled into an ever narrowing channel as the tide rises and forms the large wave. The river's course takes the Bore from around 5 miles wide to just a mile in width in a very short distance and before long it is down to a width of just a few hundred yards. By the time the river reaches Minsterworth it is less than a hundred yards across, maintaining this width all the way to Gloucester.

The word Bore was coined by the Hwicce, the Anglo-Saxon river dwellers on the Severn (interestingly the Norse equivalent of the tribal Hwicce is Viking) – and the Norse meaning bara translates as a wave or swell. The Germanic and Norse languages share many similarities and Bore and Bara are a good example of this. Its meaning boils downs to a tidal surge on a river; a single high wave of water resembling a wall.

The Bore has now become a point of focus for surfers with the world surfing record held by a Gloucestrian, well a Hempsted chap to be exact, Dave Lawson, who stayed on the surf for 5.7 miles and on his board for 35 minutes! Apart from surfers, windsurfers and canoeists also can't get enough of this unusual event when they're not messing about on the river.

Food from the river has always been in great demand: wild salmon, eels and elvers and lampreys. Lampreys are similar in shape to eels. Rather gruesomely they feed on fish flesh, like leeches clamping onto their victims, sucking out their bodily fluids and rasping away at the flesh.

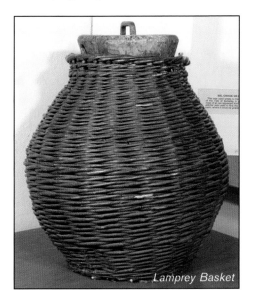
Lamprey Basket

If I now tell you lampreys were regarded by early Gloucester folks as delicacies don't squirm! Gloucester has long been famous for its lampreys. By ancient custom, the city of Gloucester, in token of its loyalty, used to present a lamprey pie annually, at Christmas, to the sovereign, the pastry generally being made out of the fat of the fish. Lampreys being at a premium and out of season, it cost a lot to send such a tasty pie to the monarch so the custom died out in 1836 except for special orders at coronations.

The Severn became famous for its lampreys, and Gloucester noted for its peculiar mode of stewing them. A well-stewed Gloucester lamprey was a luxury that was sought after. King Henry I died of ptomaine poisoning through eating the wriggly parasitic things. He became ill not long after arriving in Normandy and died on 1st December 1135 at St Denis-le-Fermont near Rouen.

So great was the demand for lamprey in the reign of King John (1167–1216) that a writ was issued to the sheriffs of Gloucester forbidding them when first landed to be sold for more than two shillings a piece. The monarch also levied a fine of 40 marks on the city of Gloucester for failing to 'pay him sufficient respect in the matter of his lampern'. It didn't do him any good as in 1216 he contracted dysentery, some say through over-eating and some say the culprits were too many lampreys, he died at just 48 years old – was it the fish or was he poisoned? The jury is still out on this.

A royal order to the sheriff in Gloucester in the 1230s declared: 'after lampreys all fish seem insipid to both the king and the queen, the sheriff shall procure by purchase or otherwise as many lampreys as possible in his bailiwick, place them in bread and jelly, and send them to the king while he is at a distance from those parts by John of Sandon, the king's cook, who is being sent to him. When the king comes nearer, he shall send them to him fresh.'

In the reign of Edward III they were sometimes sold for eightpence or ten-pence a piece, and often produced a much higher price. In 1341, Walter Dastyn, sheriff of Gloucester, received the sum of £12 5s 3d for forty-four lampreys supplied for the king's use.

Queen Victoria's chef Charles Elme Francatelli wrote the following on lamprey: 'one being the sea or marine lamprey, which is abundant at Gloucester and Worcester, where it is dressed and preserved for the purpose of being given as presents. The lamprey is considered to be in best condition during the month of April and May when it ascends the Severn from the sea for the purpose of depositing its spawn.'

Eels and elvers are best caught at night and close to the banks where the water swills and froths at speed against the land. Just before a Bore arrives men are stationed along the riverbank and in chain-reaction fashion the alarm goes up as to how far it has progressed. Nets are put into the water with the open mouth facing downstream and the fish are caught as they swim against the flow.

Elvers are closely related to the lamprey and can be caught as far north in the river as Tewkesbury – in some Severnside villages such as Frampton there were even elver-eating contests. Between the great wars, in the 1930s, elvers were still being caught in the Severn and sold by fish-criers throughout the city streets. They have become much more scarce, so much so the price has been hiked to astronomical realms and they are controlled in breeding stations along the river. One reason the price is so high is that many are shipped live for breeding for sushi in Japan, China and also over to Ulster to be smoked. But fear not as the Severn and Wye Smokery on the edge of the Forest of Dean smokes not just eels but salmon too.

The low-lying Severn valley is also conducive for cheese-making and Double and Single Gloucester goes down a treat to this day. Way back in time, in the 1300s Gloucester cheeses were sent to nuns in Caen, Normandy; obviously Brie and Camembert gave way to Gloucester in this instance.

The Severn was an industrial artery with iron being sourced at the Forest of Dean and Robinswood Hill. From tributaries of the Severn, little boats enabled the mineral to be sailed into Gloucester Quay. Kings as far back as Edward the Confessor used Gloucester iron as the city manufactured everything from horseshoes to nails; they were sent all over the country, exported to the Continent and undoubtedly kept the horses' hooves protected all the way to the Crusades.

Gloucester's giant castle was built on the banks of the Severn *circa* 1110, perfect for transporting men, weapons, explosives, food and drink in and out of the place.

The quay during the Saxon period was located where the third arm of the river coursed through the city to the north of Westgate Street. When the channel silted up a later river quay was constructed and is first mentioned in 1390 during the reign of King Richard II. This enabled Gloucester to take ships of around 10–30 tonnes and they could sail as far as Worcester and Shrewsbury upstream and down to Chepstow and Bristol. But the world became the city's oyster when good old Queen Bess awarded a charter giving Gloucester port status and from that time on ships could sail legitimately in and out from the seven seas into the Severn. This meant a customs house was built in 1581 most probably on the same site as the current 18th-century building.

With Queen Elizabeth's charter came port prosperity, the height of trade coming in the late 1700s when Britain had a burgeoning network of colonies springing up worldwide.

It wasn't long before Gloucester needed to improve its river communications due to problems with river restrictions that meant bigger ships could only reach the city on the highest of spring tides. This led to the idea of a canal to increase trade and be less reliant on the elements. Welcome the Berkeley or Sharpness to Gloucester canal.

This was water-breaking stuff as the proposal was to link the River Thames to the River Severn thereby opening up trade with Oxford, London and beyond, and vice versa through to Gloucester and English Midlands. In 1793 work began on 17 miles of canal but money had run out by 1800 with only 8 miles completed! It was 17 years later before work was resumed after the British had beaten the French at Waterloo, by which time Berkeley had been dropped in favour of entering the river at Sharpness reducing work by about a mile, and in 1827, 30 years later and a mile shorter it was complete.

During this time the docks weren't idle as a graving dock was given the go-ahead in 1818. This is where a ship can be repaired. Once the ship is in the graving dock the water can be pumped out, giving access to below the water line. 'Graving' means 'scratching', somewhere you went to scratch off barnacles, rust and anything that can be hazardous to the ship or slow it down in the water.

With the repeal of the Corn Laws a new dock was added called, as everything else was at this time, the Victoria Dock after Her Madge. It was also known as the Salt Basin as salt had been a precious commodity since time immemorial and with the major saline town, Droitwich, upriver in Worcestershire it made it easy to transport the precious white stuff to Gloucester Docks and the world beyond, most especially to other parts of the British Isles.

Gloucester was hosting seamen of all nations so a Mariners' Chapel was built. On Sundays during the first half of the 1800s the dock gates were closed and church was the main focus of all God-fearing souls. However, it was not considered right and proper that salty old sailors should mix with the city folks so in 1849 the quaint Mariners' Chapel was opened and what happened? All the city folks went there!

St Nicholas at the Bridge church was always known as the sailor's church long before the wee chapel was opened. St Nicholas is the patron saint of sailors as well as dockers, fishermen and Father Christmases everywhere! It originally guarded the new bridge built across the river in the 12th century. The parish included part of the medieval quayside on the third arm of the Severn which has now silted up and vanished and of course long since moved to its present position.

One of the highlights of my visit to the city was a trip around the Docks on a delightful little boat, the *Queen Boadicea II*, famous in her own selfless right for leaving the safety of the Severn and heading across the dangerous waters of the English Channel at the mercy of Nazi dive bombers at Dunkirk on her mission to rescue the brave soldiers of Britain in World War II. You simply must take a trip on her, so much history on the

decks of one little boat; we owe her so much, and she looks so smart since her restoration in 2005. Spend time in the brilliant National Waterways Museum – don't miss it now. It is based in the Llanthony Warehouse built in 1850 and tells you everything you ever needed to know about, well, British Waterways and of course the great river that is the life blood of this great city.

Queen Boadicea II was built as a sturdy passenger boat, with a 65ft all-steel hull. Her 3ft draft was just fine for the River Thames, where she started working life when her mistress, Mrs C M Smith, used to ply between Westminster and Greenwich in 1936. This spunky little vessel was fine and fit to sail across the notoriously fickle English Channel providing the weather and sea remained calm but not for crossing it on a bad day.

But if you're a boat called the *Boadicea* the spirit of the warrior Queen of the Iceni's namesake was bound to shine through and rise to any challenge which is precisely what happened on Friday 31st May 1940. Trapped on the beaches and shores of Dunkirk the soldiers of the British Expeditionary Force were gradually being hemmed in by Nazi planes and panzer divisions and when the cry for help went up our British servicemen had their backs to the sea. A call to arms was sent to the boats of Britain to come to the rescue. From all over the country the call was answered by a motley crew of wonderful little crafts of every shape and size with hearts as big as the *QE2*.

Boadicea II was one of the heroic boats that answered the SOS and headed to the still calm waters of the Thames where they were to muster at Twickenham and Teddington in Middlesex, from there they would head out passing the City of London and into the unpredictable swell of the North Sea.

On the day a fresh on-shore breeze developed. *QBII*, commanded by Lieutenant J S Seal, RNR, avoided the beaches due to dangerous conditions from sky and sea and made straight for Dunkirk harbour. There she met heavy shelling made worse by enemy air attacks from the German dive bombers and fighters.

Boadicea arrived to see the heart wrenchingly tragic loss of the motor boat Janice, working off Dunkirk pier, demolished by a direct hit from a bomb. Her skipper Sub-Lieut. Bell, RNVR, was killed, together with a stoker rating. The *QBII* managed to pick up three of Janice's crew who were thrown into the water as she went down. In total a lucky 13 soldiers were rescued from Dunkirk thanks to the brave *QBII*.

She made her way back through the choppy waters avoiding the menacing cluster of Nazi aircraft, like steel grey birds of prey ready to swoop down and kill.

You know as I write this my eyes are filling up, no really – call it pride, sadness, whatever it is, it gets you right here. Now you can pay your respects to this heroine by supporting her in her dotage as she takes it nice 'n' easy along the Gloucester and Sharpness Canal three times a day. Don't you think this second warrior queen deserves it? Something to tell your friends and family.

In 1980 four hundred years after Gloucester gained port status, HRH the Duke of Gloucester declared the celebrations for Port 400 well and truly open. And to show the age-old attraction that living by water brings even the city council moved to the North Warehouse at the Docks. As you read this the Docks are going through a massive gentrification to make it one of the most upmarket places to live in Gloucester.

The River Severn and its waters remain a part and parcel of Gloucester.

CHARLES II
This statue was carved in 1662 by Stephen Baldwyn
and was set up in the Wheat Market in Southgate Street.
It was removed in the middle of the nineteenth century
and its whereabouts remained obscure until 1945 when
it was re-discovered in pieces in a garden at Chas Hill.
Re-erected in this position, 1960

" it wasn't long before the Cavaliers
appeared on the horizon ready for action "

Gloucester Siege

Understanding Gloucester's geographical position as the lowest bridging point on the River Severn and its fine highway position between London, Oxford and Wales, and the North and Midlands with Wales and the South West, gives you the explicit reasons why it is a very attractive prize for any invader who wants to secure the West of England and Wales.

This was no secret, especially to the good folks of Gloucester who in August 1642 formed a Defence Council and the mayor ordered the city gates to be locked between 9pm and sunrise. By the autumn the city came out in full support for Oliver Cromwell and Parliament and became a fiercely loyal stronghold for the Roundheads under the precocious leadership of the 23-year-old Governor Edward Massey (or Massie) who entered the city complete with an infantry and two troops of horse. Gloucester was asking for trouble with such defiant action as King Charles and his army needed the city to win the war, especially considering Bristol and shire were under King and Crown and only this great city was playing hard to get. The urgency for capture was increased as Parliament held only two other ports – Plymouth and Hull – emphasizing Gloucester's importance to both sides.

The city's proximity to the Forest of Dean, which had useful iron ore deposits but was under Royalist control, made it necessary for the Gloucester Garrison to keep enemy troops in check and prevent them breaking out in the direction of the city and beyond with supplies.

It was early in1643 that Colonel Massey pulled together his inadequate defence force of around 1700 men and horse; he called on all willing hands to repair the city's Roman walls and castle and throw up earthworks to protect Gloucester.

It wasn't long before the Cavaliers appeared on the horizon ready for action and to seize the city. As the king's army drew closer the town clerk ordered that the priory church tower be demolished to deny the king's men a vantage point that could be used as a viewfinder to aim their guns.

The king stationed himself at Matson House about two miles to the southeast of the city, and guaranteed Gloucestrians a pardon if they came over to his side. Any thought of surrender was anathema and blatantly refused. To prove how much Gloucester ranked as a cherished desire to Charles I he gave the offensive and initiative to his nephew, the dashing Prince Rupert of the Rhine, who stationed himself at Prinknash Park just over four miles to the southeast. The two sides lined up thus: King – around 30,000 men and artillery v Parliament – 1700 men including horse; the siege of Gloucester began on 10th August 1643.

If it wasn't for the weather, unusually bad for August, the king's troops would have undermined the city walls via the tunnels they had dug. Those villages, farms and buildings outside the walls that hadn't been destroyed by Parliament to prevent them becoming refuge to the Royalists, were now taken by the king whose men had also knocked out the city's water supply from Robinswood Hill.

The City's representatives answer the King's demands for Gloucester to surrender, 10th August 1643, painted in 1865 by Robert Dowling

Word was despatched to Roundhead top dog, the Earl of Essex, back in London, that Gloucester was under siege, and his force was needed to relieve and save the city. Without further ado 15,000 militia went west and by 5th September the king and his men had heard the earl was already at Cheltenham and with a feeling of desolation soon left their post and withdrew to Painswick. By the 6th it was all over, Gloucester was back carrying on Parliamentary business.

That was Gloucester's moment of Civil War glory complete, apart from a few odds and ends. Its garrison remained alert and ready if called upon. On 22nd April 1645 Prince Rupert faced a force from Gloucester at Ledbury, Herefordshire and won. In May, Evesham was wrested from the king by the Gloucester Garrison under siege hero Edward Massey. During March 1646 the combined Evesham and Gloucester garrisons proved too much for Lord Astley on his way to the king at Oxford,

his lordship was completely overwhelmed at Stow on the Wold on 20th March and by the morning of the 21st he had surrendered and his army dispersed.

Cromwell visited the city in 1648 en route for Wales but as to where he fed and watered is unknown. In 1651 the Royalists rose again as Charles made another attempt to take back his throne, this time at Worcester. Gloucester's rulers continued to support Cromwell sending guns, food and ale, and after the victory a gift of lampreys (eel-like delicacies from the River Severn).

In July 1657 Oliver Cromwell was declared Lord Protector but despite support for Parliament the city was inches away from losing its greatest treasure, the cathedral. The Puritans thought it cost far too much and didn't bring in enough to warrant its existence! Thank goodness their short-sightedness didn't prevail considering how many visitors it brings to this fine city, to this day. The then Bishop of Gloucester,

Godfrey Goodman, left before the religious iconoclasts could set about their destruction – the Roundheads did manage to take as much as they could from his own house, however. That's twice the cathedral was saved, once by Henry VIII and now by the people.

Come 1660 with the Civil War ended, the Republic was abandoned and Restoration celebrated. Despite a vow of allegiance from the city's rulers, Gloucester was to bear the brunt of Royal revenge. All those defences that had protected the city against the crown were destroyed in 1661; the walls, gates and the massive Norman castle were flattened.

In 1662, as if to keep his eye on the city, a statue of Charles II was unveiled at the northern end of the Wheat Market in Southgate Street and now stands rather worse for wear in Three Cocks Lane. Before it lost its lustre it certainly had the desired effect on Edward Massey who left Cromwell's cause due to idealistic differences between himself and Parliament and joined with Charles. He went to Scotland on behalf of the king and fought for him against his former Puritan masters, being wounded at Upton upon Severn just before the Battle of Worcester. Afterwards he escaped to France.

Charles II became King of Scotland and England on 29th May 1660. Massey returned to Gloucester just before in April 1660 and was elected MP for the city – although not unanimously by any means – he was eventually knighted by a grateful Charles and became Governor of Jamaica.

The bases of the East Gate Tower and adjacent ditches have been revealed through excavation and it's really worth taking a look inside the glass-topped structure in Eastgate Street.

The churches of St Mary de Lode and Holy Trinity were used as prisons during the war and St Mary de Crypt an ammunition dump.

By the way don't be taken in by the sign on the corner of 26 Westgate Street and Maverdine Lane that wrongly states Edward Massie was installed here during the Siege, my good friend Phil Moss, Mr Gloucester, tells me that he wasn't! It may have been the next road down and someone must have miscalculated.

However, the building in question which has served many purposes including an Assize Judge's lodgings is quite superb; a glorious timber-framed house built in the 1500s, four storeys high and undoubtedly one of the finest examples of its kind anywhere. It is best viewed from the inside by popping into the shop and up the stairs and outside by going down Maverdine Lane and looking up: enjoy.

Glorious Glosters

The Soldiers of Gloucester, City and County.

At the end of World War 1 the Gloucestershire Regiment was comprised of six battalions. Three of these, the 1st, 2nd and 5th, were known as 'Pals' regiments as they consisted entirely of County and City men, very often from the same streets and villages, who fought and died together in the carnage of the hell-hole called the Great War.

These brave soldiers entered the most murderous war in human history under their new names, the 1st and 2nd Battalions known originally as the 28th (raised in 1694) and 61st (raised in 1758) Regiments of Foot. The 1st Battalion was in the thick of the fight from the very beginnings of

battle almost to its close. The 2nd Battalion was in China on the eve of war in August 1914, but was in action on the Western Front before the year was out.

Many changes occurred between the Wars so when the Second World War broke out, the 1st Royal Gloucestershire Hussars remained on the home front as a Training and Home Defence Regiment. In 1945 they were ordered to prepare to fight in the Far East theatre, against the Japanese. However the Pacific War ended in the August and in 1946 they were sent to Austria as a part of the occupying force.

In 1941, The 2nd Regiment, as part of 22 Armoured Brigade, embarked for Egypt to join the 8th Army. During the desert campaign against Field Marshall Erwin Rommel, the Regiment distinguished itself on many occasions but suffered heavy losses. General Norrie, in writing to the Brigade Commander, said, 'I always told you that you had the best Brigade in the Army. The 11th Hussars which has been in all the campaigns out here say they have never seen men fight like yours.'

On 6th June 1942 the Regiment fought its final battles as 2nd Royal Gloucestershire Hussars at an area called The Cauldron, south of Tobruk. During these actions they won no less than ten Battle Honours. Individuals had won over twenty decorations for gallantry, with several NCOs being commissioned in the field.

But where did all this Gloucester military history begin? I don't want to go through all the battles and wars the Gloucesters have taken part in, as that would distract you from visiting the fine museum dedicated to the Soldiers of Gloucestershire. There is so much for you to discover and enjoy doing it. So here is a potted history:

Since they were first formed three hundred years ago the Gloucesters have a singularly distinguished record and one of the longest lists of Battle Honours of all County Regiments; fourteen alone were won in the Peninsula War when the British and their Spanish and Portuguese allies took on Napoleon in Iberia.

The Duke of Wellington made special mention of the 28th (he only named four commendations all told!) due to their gallantry at Quatre Bras. Two days before Waterloo the 28th had to hold back wave-upon-wave of French cavalry at their defence position on the Charleroi road, known as Quatre Bras. At about 5 o'clock in the afternoon the 28th braced itself for one huge headlong massive charge of dextrous Polish Lancers and cuirassier veterans led by the famous Marshal Ney, and the Gloucesters successfully resisted the onslaught.

The 61st was nicknamed the Flowers of Toulouse, for bravery displayed and heavy losses endured at the Battle of Toulouse in 1814. In a violent and vicious attack against the French commanded by Marshal Soult, Napoleon's most able Marshal, they drove the Frenchies back to the suburbs of Toulouse. Due to the great number of dead soldiers scattered in their scarlet tunics on the field of battle they became known as the Flowers of Toulouse: a tribute to their bravery.

The Royal Gloucestershire Hussars aka the Yeomanry appeared on the scene in 1795 along with another volunteer cavalry regiment in 1795; both were ready to repel a possible French invasion which the Government was sure was on the cards. Men from the City of Gloucester were part and parcel of the recruitment but it was a false call to arms so they were all stood down in 1802 and disbanded.

But when the cards were reversed and Britain declared war on Napoleon in 1803 they were reformed along with four additional troops. The Gloucester City Troop was commanded by a rich and influential banker, Robert Morris, who lived at Barnwood Court and was MP for the City; the election was said to have cost him a cool fifty grand!

By 1813 – two years before Waterloo – there were eleven battalions in Gloucestershire with a total of 582 officers and their men. By 1834 they were combined into a single regiment and on 21st April the Marquis of Worcester was gazetted Lieutenant Colonel Commandant of the Gloucestershire Yeomanry Cavalry. Like other Yeomanry they had been enrolled for home guard duty only. In 1810 they were called out to quell riots in Gloucester city itself. Hardly the kind of training to cope with what fate had in store.

The 5th Battalion was a Territorial Unit, directly descended from the several Volunteer Corps raised in different parts of the county in 1859 and enrolled as the County Corps in 1860. Under the Cardwell scheme they were given the title, the Second Volunteer Battalion of the Gloucestershire Regiment in 1881 and the 5th under the Haldane Scheme in 1908. Gloucester was the HQ. Although formed for home duties the Battalion was awarded the South African Battle Honour for services rendered in the Boer War.

Now here are a couple of battles that I think show the true grit of the Gloucesters:

In 1801, the 28th Foot (North Gloucester-shire) under the Command of General Sir Ralph Abercromby landed in Egypt and prepared to fight the French at the port city of Alexandria.

The Regiment took up a defensive position on a line of low sand hills. To their right an old Roman fort standing on a slight rise close to the shore; to the front an unfinished redoubt, manned by the good old boys of 28th. Between them, the fort and the redoubt formed the key position for if either was taken then the British flank could be turned.

Under the cover of early morning darkness and sand dunes, two columns of French infantry headed straight for the British right. Heavy fighting ensued and as more French columns joined the attack the 28th was cut off. British rifles drove off the French barrage but a brigade of French infantry moved through the gap between the 28th and the rest of the British line.

A counter attack by the 42nd Foot, the Black Watch Royal Highlanders, drove off the attack but they went too far and were now also in danger from French cavalry. The battle raged all along the line, but nowhere as fiercely as on the right, with the 28th fighting to their front and flanks. More French cavalry joined in, supported by even more infantry. Some of the cavalry broke through the 42nd and formed up to charge the 28th in the rear. With no reserves available at this critical point in the battle, Lt. Col. Chambers, who had taken over command following the serious wounding of the C.O. Col. Paget, gave the now legendary order 'Rear rank, 28th! Right about face!'

The rear ranks turned and with amazing discipline waited until the French cavalry were a few horse strides away. They then fired a devastating volley, causing heavy casualties amongst the cavalry and forcing the enemy to retreat and withdraw. For their gallantry in fighting back to back, the Regiment was given the unique honour of wearing a badge at the back of their caps. This honour prevails: The Battle Honour 'Egypt' with the Sphinx together with the laurel leaves of victory are also on the Regimental Colour. Back Badge Day is celebrated every 21st March.

One other of many extraordinary events occurred in the Korean War in the 1950s. A hundred and thirty-six years after their commendation by none other than Hooky Nose himself, the Duke of Wellington, the Regiment was about to win their most famous nickname. It began when they were ordered to hold Hill 235 above the Imjin River in Korea.

In 1951 the Chinese Army swarmed like ants across the Korean border to take on the fledgling United Nations Army. But the UN troops, led by the USA, were soon retreating south. The Gloucesters were to hold a line above the Imjin River to give time for the other brigades to pass by, sacrificing themselves if need be. An endless stream of Chinese soldiers appeared on the horizon, homing in on the Gloucesters and fired up by a constant cacophony of bugles. On Hill 235 the guns grew so hot they seized up and stalled, but the enemy never stopped coming at the Gloucester boys, hurling

themselves into the fray. It didn't matter that they were an untrained ragbag army, just their sheer weight of numbers was terrifying enough.

To counter the fearful noise of the Chinese bugles, one fine Lieutenant ordered the Drum-Major to reply with regimental tunes and trumpet calls. Only 39 young Gloucester men survived on the hill that day. And the name that resounded across and around the world – **The Glorious Glosters**, that says it all. Enough said.

A postscript to the heroic stand at the Battle of Imjin River: One Colonel JP Carne was captured in December 1951 and during his imprisonment in Korea he carved a stone cross; it is beautiful in its simplicity and is in its rightful place in the North Ambulatory of Gloucester Cathedral.

On 27th April 1994 it was the end of an honourable era; a new Regiment entered the Order of Battle of the British Army when the Gloucestershire Regiment and the Duke of Edinburgh's Royal Regiment (Berkshire & Wiltshire) merged. They are stationed in my own dear home County of Middlesex at Hounslow, itself one of the regimental towns of the Middlesex Regiment – and proud we are indeed to have such illustrious guests on our soil as the Glorious Glosters.

For more information go to the website: *www.glosters.org.uk/*

Gloster Aircraft

This remarkable part of Britain, like Malta, deserves a medal for these two places forged two ends of a common World War II bond.

1921 Gloster Mars / 1922 Gloster Sparrowhawk / 1923 Gloster Grebe / 1923 Gloster Grouse / 1925 Gloster Gamecock / 1934 Gloster Gauntlet / 1934 Gloster Gladiator 1937 Gloster F.5/34 monoplane fighter prototype / 1939 Gloster F.9/37 twin-engined heavy fighter prototype / 1941 Gloster E.28/39 first British jet engineered aircraft / 1944 Gloster Meteor / 1948 Gloster E.1/44 1954 Gloster Javelin and the Mars, Gannet, Gambet, Gorcock, Guan, Goral and Gnatsnapper / Gloster also built the Hawker Henley light bomber in 1939 plus 1,000 Hurricanes in the first 12 months of WWII. The last of the 2,750 Hurricanes built at Brockworth were delivered to the RAF in March 1942. In 1942, production started on 3,330 Typhoons for the RAF.

Gloster Mars I racer of 1923 painted by C.E.P. Davis who was production development engineer at Gloster Aircraft Company until 1962

Think of Gloster aeroplanes and I bet you automatically see the Gloster Gladiator. These plucky little aircraft captured the imagination of almost everyone with their derring-do during World War II. There is something so Boy's Own about the RAF's last combative biplane design, taking gingerly to the air in a modern war when sexy fighter planes like the Hurricane and Spitfire were beating a path to the German's door, themselves soon to be out-stripped by jet planes doing much of what they did more quickly!

Not so long ago I watched a TV documentary and discovered that Gloucester, Hucclecote and Brockworth were at the heart of some of the most ingenious aviation design and progress. This part of Britain pioneered the jet engine with its test runway famous for the first flight of a jet plane.

The Gloster Aircraft Company was founded in 1915 as the Gloucestershire Aircraft Company Limited. The company acquired a 50 per cent stake of its component supplier HH Martyn aircraft business and Aircraft Manufacturing Company the other half. The company rented what was the Sunningend works of HH Martyn. By 1917, the GAC was producing large numbers of fuselage and spares; this is when the historic Belfast Hangars were constructed. As orders for aircraft increased work was subcontracted out locally.

When any flying was scheduled planes were moved seven miles by road to the Air Board aircraft acceptance park at Hucclecote. By the end of World War I, the company was able to produce 45 complete aircraft a week. With the changeover to metal construction, the Sunningend factory was no longer suitable and in 1928, the company – which since 1926 was officially named the Gloster Aircraft Company Limited as overseas clients could not get their tongue round its name – bought the aerodrome at Hucclecote, complete with hangars and offices.

Gloster Grebe fighter of 1923 painted by C.E.P. Davis who was production development engineer at Gloster Aircraft Company until 1962

The Chief Designer of the Gloster Aircraft Company, H.P. Folland originally from the old Nieuport Company, helped produce the high-speed, single-seat biplane the 'Bamel' in 1921. By 1922, it held the world air-speed record set at 212.15 mph.

In 1922, GAC received its first international order: 50 Sparrowhawks for the Imperial Japanese Navy.

The first Gloster monoplane – the Gloster VI called the 'Golden Arrow' – broke the world speed record at 336.31 mph on 10th September 1929. With global recession in the early 1930s, the company diversified and manufactured everything from fish-fryers to steel milk churns as well as metal roll-up shop fronts and motor car bodies.

In September 1933, the SS19 was selected to produce the Gloster Gauntlet for the RAF. Folland's team therefore began to examine possible further refinements to the Gauntlet design.

In May 1934, Gloster Aircraft was bought by Hawker Aircraft Limited, and this introduced substantial financial capital and aircraft structures knowledge. The maiden flight took place on 12th September 1934. On 1st July 1935 the name Gladiator was officially announced and an initial contract for 23 aircraft placed. The Gloster Gladiator was to become the last British biplane fighter. In September 1935 a second order for 180 aircraft was agreed. The first export contract was to Latvia on 27th May 1937.

At the end of 1937 the Royal Navy began to show interest in a shipboard version of the Gladiator II as a replacement for the Hawker Nimrod. The Sea Gladiator was the variant adopted by the Fleet Air Arm. 22 Gladiator Mk II's built at Brockworth were supplied as interim Sea Gladiators and enrolled in December 1938. The Sea Gladiator saw action with Fleet Air Arm squadrons from 1938, but first embarked aboard HMS *Courageous* with 801 Squadron in March 1939 as well as 802 Squadron of the FAA aboard HMS *Glorious* and 804 Squadron attached to HMS *Furious* but operating from Hatston, Orkney; both saw action off the coast of Norway.

Gloster Gauntlet fighter of 1933 painted by C.E.P. Davis who was production development engineer at Gloster Aircraft Company until 1962

Carrier-based Sea Gladiators were more successful since their slower speed made them more suitable for such marine operations and they were less likely to face more modern fighter opposition.

At the beginning of the war the Gloster Gladiators serving with the FAA were primarily used as carrier-borne fighters. However, with their replacement by faster and more modern fighters they were found excellent for useful duties such as communications, liaison and meteorological reconnaissance aircraft.

The Gladiator was used during WWII in theatres where the RAF or FAA had no other means of air combat. The Gladiator took part in the Norwegian campaign in 1940, and was victorious in 1940–41 during the first campaigns in the Mediterranean; it was particularly active in the defence of Crete in May 1941.

But it was on the island of Malta where the Gladiator became legendary. The Royal Navy had stored a number of Sea Gladiators in crates to re-supply carrier squadrons as required. There was a stock of 18 aircraft remaining at Malta after HMS *Glorious* was sunk. Many aircraft were shipped in crates, one of the reasons why pilots used to call them 'old crates'.

In May 1940, four Sea Gladiators were assembled by the RAF and test flown. For 10 days from 11th to 21st June, the Sea Gladiators represented the tiny island's sole air defence. The Italians staged only three air raids on the island during this period before Hurricanes were sent as relief. Due to a shortage of ammunition, the Sea Gladiators were used to break up bomber formations, rather than pick off individual targets.

Months later, a Maltese newspaper published a report on the Sea Gladiators which ensured that the names Faith, Hope and Charity (although never actually applied to the aircraft) entered Maltese history and aviation legend. They were part of the Hal Far Fighter Flight. Sea Gladiator N5520 joined in April 1940. She was quick to defend Malta, and piloted by Flt Lt JL Waters RAF shot down and destroyed an Italian S.79 on 11th June 1940, and the next day on 12th June 1940 destroyed another S.79. She was renamed 'Faith' between October 1941 and January 1942. Her fuselage has been preserved for posterity by the grateful Maltese and can be seen to this day in the Malta Aviation Museum.

Sea Gladiator N5531 was renamed 'Hope' on 19th April 1940 but was destroyed in an air raid on 4th February 1941. Sea Gladiator N5519, 'G6A' of 802 Squadron from June–September 1939, was renamed 'Charity' on 19th April 1940. She was involved in defending Malta over the critical 1940 period but was shot down on 29th July 1940 and her pilot F/O PW Hartley RAF was badly burned.

The Gloster Gladiator was, as the famous test-pilot Captain Eric M. Brown said *'undoubtedly one of the greatest biplane fighters ever built, but, appearing almost simultaneously with the first of the new breed of heavily armed monoplane fighters and bombers, it was pitched into a combat era where it was out-gunned and outperformed, though never out-manoeuvred'.*

When Germany invaded Norway on 9th April 1940 No. 263 Squadron was flown to Norway to assist British forces against a German invasion. Gladiators based at Fornebu Airport, consisting of seven operational biplanes, managed to shoot down a total of five German aircraft with only one Gladiator being shot down. Operations from the frozen Lake Lesjaskag ended when Luftwaffe bombers destroyed the aircraft on the ground.

Gloster Gladiator fighter of 1935 painted by C.E.P. Davis who was production development engineer at Gloster Aircraft Company until 1962

Replacement Gladiators accompanied the Squadron when it was deployed to Narvik in the far north. They fought continuously until 7th June, claiming 26 confirmed victories, before the survivors landed on HMS *Glorious* for the voyage home. The carrier was subsequently attacked by the German battle-cruisers *Scharnhorst* and *Gneisenau* and sunk.

Two Gladiator squadrons, 607 and 615, headed to France as part of the British Expeditionary Force in 1939. In just ten days of hard fighting following the opening of the German assault on 10th May 1940, they were destroyed. In a desperate attempt to provide fighter cover for the evacuation of Dunkirk, a detachment of Gladiators known

as 'G' Flight was formed at RAF Manston (now Kent International airport) in late May. Then when the Battle of Britain was being fought only two home-based units used the Gladiator operationally.

When Italy entered the war in June 1940, Gladiators were serving with Nos. 33 and 80 Squadrons in Egypt, and with No. 94 Squadron in Aden. The Gladiator proved an even match for the Fiat CR.42 and was successful in helping repel the Italian invasion of Egypt and defeat Italian forces in East Africa.

Gladiators participated in the Greek campaign, achieving good results against the Regia Aeronautica. Greek Gladiators destroyed many Italian aircraft in 1940 and 1941, as well as some German aircraft during the 1941 invasion, but were outclassed once the Luftwaffe joined the battle.

In 1941, Gladiators from No. 94 Squadron participated in the 'Battle of Habbaniyah' against Iraqi rebels besieging the RAF training base. Iraqi Gladiators were flown in sorties against British and Indian forces in 1941. The Iraqis used them until 1949 for ground attack missions against the Kurds. Gladiators continued to serve in the Western Desert throughout 1941, but finally disappeared from front line service in January 1942.

Irish Gladiators shot down several British barrage balloons that had broken from their moorings. Belgian Gladiators suffered heavy losses to the Germans in 1940.

The first export aircraft to see combat were those of the Chinese Government, which had acquired 36 Gladiator Mk I's for use against the invading Japanese. Despite numerous accidents by inexperienced pilots, the survivors flew with some success in the defence of Siu-Chow during 1938. In the Far East, the Gladiator fared little better against Japanese aircraft. It played a part in the short-lived defence of Singapore.

In Swedish service the Gladiator I was designated J 8, and the Gladiator II designated J 8A. Some of these served with Flygflottilj 19, the volunteer unit that flew alongside the Finnish Air Force in the Winter War of 1939–40. The Swedish unit was in action for 62 days, destroying six Russian bombers and six fighters for the loss of three Gladiators – one due to an accident.

Many RAF Gladiators were gifted to Allied forces including Greece, South Africa and Egypt. The Royal Egyptian Air Force aircraft remained airworthy until shortly after the end of the war, whilst Portugal retained its Gladiators for advanced pilot training until 1953 before scrapping them.

L8032 is the only airworthy Gloster Gladiator in the world and was the last Gladiator I to come off the production line.

Built by the Gloster Aircraft Company in 1937 it was first posted to No 2 Anti-Aircraft Co-operation Unit and used to assist in training anti-aircraft gunners. After the war, L8032 was entered in a few races and later used as a civil aircraft before being returned to the Gloster Aircraft Company on 23rd February, 1948, exactly eleven years after the first Mk I made its way to 72 Squadron. Rebuilt, refitted with 303 Browning machine guns and re-painted with RAF markings, L8032 can be seen along with the sole surviving airworthy Gladiator maintained and preserved by the Shuttleworth Trust at Old Warden, Bedfordshire.

Gloster's private venture development of the already highly refined Gauntlet brought the biplane fighter concept to the peak of technical perfection. In many air arms, it smoothed the transition to advanced monoplane fighters, and in confronting aircraft of its own era it performed well, but when pitted against modern combat aircraft its obsolescent design was cruelly exposed. The skill and determination of its pilots, however, has allowed the Gladiator to acquire an heroic status that could easily have become tragic.

King George VI and his devoted wife, Queen Elizabeth knew that their main job during the Second World War was to tour the country and keep the British bulldog spirit in full menacing growl! Their Majesties arrived at Gloucester in February 1940 and headed for Hucclecote to see with their own eyes construction of fighter aircraft. It was in the nick of time as by the September of the same year the Battle of Britain was in full tilt with aerial attacks and dog-fights, and helped by a few odd decisions from Berlin, showed the true worth of the machines and pilots as being in a class of their own to overcome the Goering's Luftwaffe.

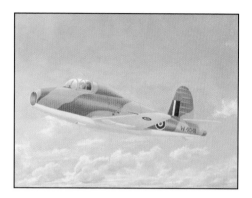

Gloster E.28/39 experimental plane of 1940 painted by C.E.P. Davis who was production development engineer at Gloster Aircraft Company until 1962

Gloster Javelin Mk.8 jet fighter of 1950–8 painted by C.E.P. Davis who was production development engineer at Gloster Aircraft Company until 1962

On 8th April 1941, the first test flight of the Gloster E.28/39, with a turbo-jet engine invented by Sir Frank Whittle took off from the company's airfield at Hucclecote. This formed the basis for the Gloster Meteor, the only jet used by the Allied Forces during World War II. The Gloster Meteor was the first operational Allied jet fighter aircraft of World War II first flying with the British Royal Air Force (RAF) in 1943. The Meteor commenced operations in mid-1944, only some weeks later than the world's first operational jet, the German Messerschmitt Me 262.

In 1945, a Gloster F.4 Meteor prototype, stripped of armament, gained a World Speed Record of 606 mph with Group Captain H. Wilson at the controls.

In early 1946, another F.4 prototype set a world air speed record of 616 mph, Group Captain 'Teddy' Donaldson flying the highly modified Meteor, nicknamed 'Yellow Peril'. Meteors remained in service with several air forces for many years and saw action with the Royal Australian Air Force in the Korean War.

Eventually, Gloster Meteors in fighter, trainer and night fighter versions were in operational use by 12 nations.

It was realised that the British Isles could be threatened by bombers flying at high altitudes and dropping their bombs through cloud cover guided by means of radar. As a result, the Javelin was developed as a two seater all-weather fighter, which could fly

faster than the speed of sound and reach altitudes above 50,000 feet. With its characteristic delta shape the Javelin was awarded super-priority production in July 1952.

This modern aircraft was too heavy to take off from the short airfield in Hucclecote, and so was kitted out to the bare minimum and a very small fuel load. It was then flown in a short hop to RAF Moreton Valence three miles to the south, where the aircraft would be completed. Parts of this old airfield can still be seen as you drive on the M5 motorway just south of Junction 12. The motorway was constructed parallel to the runway and at either end, large concrete sections of taxiway can be seen angling off the carriageway.

It was this shortcoming of the facilities, along with the rationalisation of the British aircraft industry that would lead to the demise of the Gloster Aircraft Company.

Gloster Meteor F8 jet fighter of 1943–7 painted by C.E.P. Davis who was production development engineer at Gloster Aircraft Company until 1962

In 1961, the company was merged with Sir W G Armstrong Whitworth Aircraft Limited to form Whitworth Gloster Aircraft Limited. Due to a lack of further orders from Her Majesty's Government, the Gloster Aircraft Company closed in 1962.

Following another re-organisation by the owners, the Hawker Siddeley Group, the firm became part of the Avro Whitworth Division of Hawker Siddeley Aviation in 1963, and the name Gloster disappeared. The site at Hucclecote was sold in 1964. The runway, while still visible from the air, has been partially obstructed by buildings on what is now the Gloucester Trading Estate. Many of the firms on it are based in the former hangars. What a story.

HMS Gloucesters

It took Oliver Cromwell and his men to commission the first
Gloucester and she wasn't even an HMS!

I presume she was named after the city to honour Gloucester's valour in holding out for Parliament against the king in the Civil War; this was, of course, still very fresh in their minds. My heart went out to the HMS *Gloucester* that became the subject of a BBC documentary because of the loss of ship and life in World War II. I have listed each of the ships that have borne the *Gloucester* name so proudly, right up to the ship that currently serves and has already made its mark on the world stage.

First HMS *Gloucester*
Oliver Cromwell 1654 to 1660,
King Charles II from 1660
Ship of the line, third rate, 70 guns
Built in 1654 as part of the great Commonwealth naval programme under Oliver Cromwell and the Rump Parliament, HMS *Gloucester* first saw action in the West Indies against Spain. She was heavily involved in the Dutch Wars, gaining six battle honours starting with the British victory in the battle of Lowestoft June 1665, followed by the Four Days Battle of the Second Dutch-British War. This was fought from 11th to 14th June, 1666 off North Foreland, Kent and remains one of the longest naval engagements in history ending in a Royal Navy defeat. She was at Orfordness when the tide turned with a British victory in August 1666. In the third Dutch-British war the British withdrew giving the Dutch a strategic victory at Solebay in June 1672, and the last major battles of that war were fought at Schooneveld in June 1673 and Texel later that year. Everything about this first Gloucester's career was dramatic.

She was wrecked off Great Yarmouth in 1682 sailing to the Port of Leith, Edinburgh, running aground due to a navigational error. Although many of the crew were lost His Royal Highness the Duke of York (later King James II) and Sir John Churchill, the Duke of Marlborough, were amongst the survivors.

Second HMS *Gloucester*
King William II (Scotland) III (England)
Frigate, fourth rate, 60 guns, 96 tonnes
The second HMS *Gloucester* was launched at Bristol in 1694. Not witness to anything particularly headline grabbing this Royal Naval vessel became a storage hulk on the River Thames at Deptford in 1706. Her most hair-raising episode came when she undertook an Atlantic voyage under Admiral Benbow, with orders to watch out for the skull and crossbones of notorious pirate Captain Kidd. She was broken up in 1731.

Third HMS *Gloucester*
Queen Anne
Frigate, fourth rate, 60 guns, 923 tonnes
Launched on the River Thames at Rotherhithe in July 1709 it took just four months before she saw action. On convoy duty near Cape Clear, County Cork she was attacked by the French on 26th October. After a fierce battle the *Gloucester* was 'reduced to a shambles' and captured by either the French ship *Achille* or *Lys*. Her captain (Balchen) was cleared of any blame and continued to serve, being knighted for his services in 1744.

Fourth HMS *Gloucester*
Queen Anne
Frigate, fourth rate, 50 guns, 714 tonnes
The fourth *Gloucester* was launched in 1711 at Deptford. She took part in two expeditions to the northerly waters of the Baltic.

Fifth HMS *Gloucester*
King George II
Frigate, fourth rate, 50 guns, 866 tonnes
Built at Sheerness in Kent in 1737, in 1740. Captain Anson led a squadron of ships on a round the world voyage which included the *Gloucester*. Having rounded treacherous Cape Horn and crossed the Pacific the ship was damaged in a storm near the island of Tinian off China in 1742. Anson had little choice but to order the destruction of the ship by fire to prevent her being captured.

Sixth HMS *Gloucester*
King George II
Frigate, fourth rate, 50 guns, 986 tonnes
She was launched in 1745 at Rotherhithe and Captain Charles Saunders was appointed Captain whilst sailing out of Sandwich, Kent. On 14th October 1747, as part of Admiral Hawkes' squadron, *Gloucester* took part in the action against the French off Ushant in Brittany and captured two ships: one Spanish and the other French. In January 1747 whilst on a cruise with, and under the orders of, Captain Cheap of HMS *Lark*, they captured a Spanish Galleon, the *Fort de Nantz*, off Madeira, en route from Havana, Cuba to Cadiz, Spain. As was usual the Spaniard was carrying a valuable cargo, estimated at 300,000 Louis, which was landed in Devon waters at Plymouth.

HMS *Gloucester*
King George III
The British North American *Gloucester* was a 10-gun brig launched in British North America on Lake Erie in 1807. She was captured by the Americans in April 1813 and destroyed by the British a few weeks later.

Seventh HMS *Gloucester*
King George III
Ship of the line, third rate, 74 guns
Built in the eventful year for France, Russia and Tchaikovsky, 1812, at Northfleet in Kent. In that same year her Captain Robert Williams was principally employed protecting convoys through the Great Belt – the Straits between the Danish islands of Zealand and Funen – a job he did for five successive seasons. He returned to Britain every winter when the Baltic was frozen. The *Gloucester* was part of a convoy to the Leeward Islands on 16th February 1814. From there he escorted the 90th regiment to Quebec and returned home with trade from Barbados in the September. The Gloucester was paid off at Sheerness soon after and in 1816 was at Chatham out of commission.

In 1822, she had a new Captain, Sir Edward William Owen, and was recommissioned under the same captain at Sheerness in March 1824. The Jamaica House of Assembly passed a vote of thanks to him for his prompt attention paid to protecting their commercial and naval interests. In 1825, Captain Joshua S. Horton took the helm at Sheerness and now came the high point of this HMS *Gloucester*'s service: to convey the Duke of Devonshire to St Petersburg in 1826 as Ambassador Extraordinary for the coronation of Czar Nicholas I. In 1828 Captain Jenkin Jones was stationed in the River Medway when HMS *Gloucester* became a guard ship. In 1831, she was downgraded at Chatham to a 50-gun vessel and was never recommissioned. The ship was eventually sold in 1884.

Eighth HMS *Gloucester*
King Edward VII
Town class light cruiser, 4800 tonnes
Launched in 1909 at Dalmuir, Dunbartonshire this *Gloucester* was one of a new breed of cruisers well armed and with steam turbines that gave a speed of 25 knots. She displayed the arms of the City of Gloucester prominently on board with many

of her company being Gloucestrians and sailed into Gloucester in January 1911. During the visit she was presented with a mascot: a terrifying bull terrier by the name of Bounce!

In August 1914 at the outbreak of the First World War, HMS *Gloucester* was in the eastern Mediterranean and sent to intercept the *Breslau*, a German light cruiser, and the *Goeben*, a battle cruiser. *Gloucester* caught the imagination of the allies for her high-speed pursuit of the Kaiser's Imperial ships even though they both managed to escape. At the end of the year this nippy ship was transferred to the British Grand Fleet at Scapa Flow, Orkney where she was based for the rest of the war. She flexed her muscles once more when taking part in the last and biggest battleship battle ever, the Battle of Jutland in 1916, with her 2 x 6 inch and 10 x 4 inch guns no doubt blazing.

Ninth HMS *Gloucester*
George VI
The Fighting 'G', flagship
of the 4th Cruiser Squadron

The ninth *Gloucester* was completed in January 1939 and launched by Alice, the Duchess of Gloucester. The ship became flagship of the 4th Cruiser Squadron attached to the East Indies Company. At the outbreak of war, the ship was stationed at Simonstown, Cape Town, South Africa until May 1940 when she joined the 7th Cruiser Squadron in the Mediterranean fleet based at Alexandria, Egypt.

In July 1940, when Italy entered the war, *Gloucester* was damaged by an Italian air attack and her Commanding Officer, Captain F R Garside CBE, was killed. Between August 1940 and May 1941, the ship was involved in many actions and her battle honours are legendary – is it any wonder she was nicknamed, The Fighting 'G'?

In May 1941, the Royal Navy was at sea preventing a German seaborne landing in force on the island of Crete. Thanks to our ships taking care of business many German transports that sailed from mainland Greece didn't reach Crete, but the Luftwaffe dive-bombers exacted a heavy toll upon the British ships, which unlike modern vessels did not have crucial air support. The *Gloucester* came under attack from up to 200 German dive-bombers as she sustained at least four heavy bomb hits and three near misses on 22nd May 1941. The RAF having been withdrawn left the ill-fated *Gloucester* and new cruiser, *Fiji* with only their own inadequate defences to protect themselves. Both ships fought valiantly until the bitter end, and bitter it was as both were sunk.

Survivors in the water were also strafed and bombed. From a ship's company of 807 men, only 84 of the cruiser's crew survived in the water until the next day after which they were imprisoned in German prisoner of war camps.

In less than a year's service in the Mediterranean, HMS *Gloucester* had won five battle honours and lost over 700 men and two COs. Admiral Sir Andrew Cunningham paid this tribute: *'Thus went the gallant Gloucester. She had endured all things, and no ship had worked harder or had had more risky tasks. She had been hit by bombs more times than any other vessel, and had always come up smiling.'*

But the story was not over as half a century after her loss HMS *Gloucester* was at the centre of controversy as revealed by television documentary. It alleged that the sinking of the *Gloucester* might have been the result of serious blunders by Royal Navy commanders.

New evidence emerged and was told by the BBC. It was originally believed that the loss of the battleship off the coast of the Greek island of Crete in 1941 was unavoidable due to the ferocity and diversity of enemy action. But the documentary *HMS Gloucester: The Untold Story*, alleged that military chiefs blundered by splitting the cruiser from the main fleet and sending her back into action. The vessel was directed away from the main fleet during the battle to help evacuate British troops when she was low on ammunition and without RAF cover, which had been withdrawn.

Naval records show that the cruiser was given orders to 'withdraw at discretion' an hour before she was sunk, but the *Gloucester* could have already been under attack at this point. Previously unpublished letters from senior officers about the sinking, state that it was 'a grave error' to deploy the *Gloucester* when she was so low on ammunition.

The fleet commander was heavily criticised for the decision and later removed from his command and sent to an office posting. It also raised questions about why, contrary to usual naval practice, rescue boats were not sent back under cover of darkness to pick up survivors.

One of the few survivors was interviewed; Mr John Stevens, 80, of South Ockendon, Essex, recalled the loss of the *Gloucester*: *'We were low in ammunition when we came under attack from around 200 Stukas [dive bombers]. The ship began sinking around 4.50pm and was gone within an hour. The tradition in the Navy is that when a ship has sunk, a vessel is sent back to pick up survivors under cover of darkness. That did not happen and we do not know why. We were picked up by Germans. I believe a fleet commander made a fatal error in taking the Gloucester away from the fleet. We were very low in ammunition and we should have withdrawn to Alexandria to refuel and get more ammunition.'*

The sinking of HMS *Gloucester* is commemorated with a stained-glass window at Gloucester Cathedral.

The Unfinished *Gloucester*
Queen Elizabeth II
A 2170-ton frigate to bear the name *Gloucester* was ordered from Portsmouth Dockyard in 1956 but later cancelled.

Tenth HMS *Gloucester*
Queen Elizabeth II
HMS *Gloucester* type 42 Destroyer, 4650 tonnes
This ship was built by Vosper Thorneycroft at Woolston, Southampton and launched on 2nd November 1982 by Her Royal Highness, The Duchess of Gloucester. The ship retains links with the Royal Gloucestershire Regiment and City of Gloucester. Her crest features a horseshoe from the City's Tudor Arms. She sailed from the UK on 30th August 1990 in support of the United Nations embargo against Iraq. Having already been on duty in the Gulf the ship escorted the first American ships to fire Tomahawk cruise missiles against the Iraqis on 17th January 1991.

On 25th February *Gloucester* was escorting the USS *Missouri* close to the Kuwaiti coast as it bombarded the shore with her 16 inch guns. In the early hours of that morning, an Iraqi Seersucker or Silkworm missile was fired against the *Missouri*. In less than 90 seconds, *Gloucester* had destroyed the Seersucker with two Sea Darts, in what proved to be the first validated, successful engagement of a missile by a missile combat at sea. *Gloucester* returned home after 208 days on 25th March 1991. During that time, her Lynx helicopter had successfully engaged and neutralised seven Iraqi naval units with Sea Skua missiles. During the 2006 Israel-Lebanon conflict HMS *Gloucester* was the first Royal Navy vessel to evacuate British nationals from Beirut, docking on 18th July 2006.

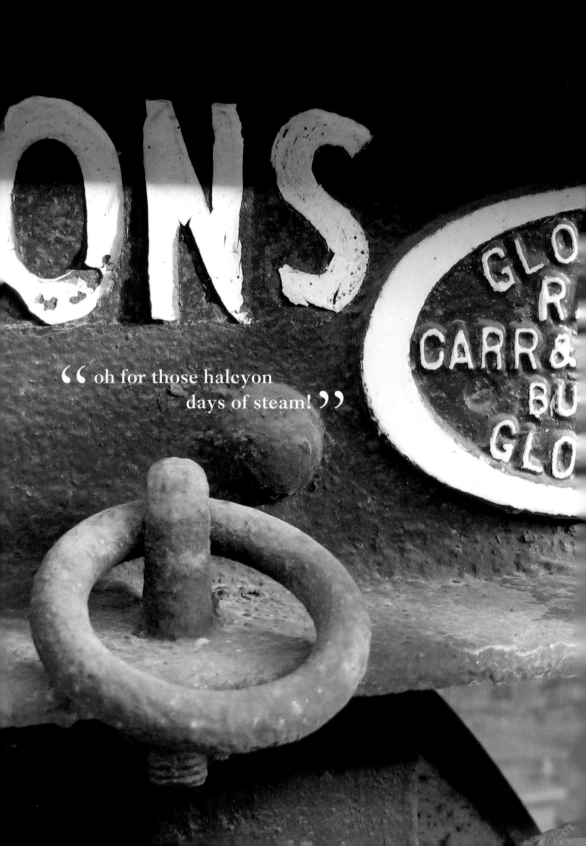

"oh for those halcyon
days of steam!"

Gloucester on the Rails

The coming of the railways was part and parcel of the
Industrial Revolution which began in the United Kingdom
and was responsible for putting another Great into Britain.

Railway fever arrived in the city on 4th
November 1840 with the Birmingham
& Gloucester Railway, which, in time,
became famous as the London Midland
Scottish Railway.

Queen Victoria was an avid user and
stopped to swap trains at Gloucester when
travelling from Balmoral (Aberdeenshire) to
Osborne House (Isle of Wight) in 1849.
She had no choice because the two
different rail companies used different
gauges! This altered in the 1870s when a
national gauge was agreed and made rail
travel so much easier.

Apart from the obvious, rails and trains,
rolling stock was in great demand and so
in 1860 Gloucester added to its incredible
transport heritage the launch of the
Gloucester Wagon Co Ltd which was
based alongside another of its travel
triumphs, the Sharpness canal. Many local
jobs were created and the first order came
from up the road with 1000 coal wagons
for the West Midlands Railway Company;
the first home order for carriages was
contracted by the London, Chatham and
Dover Railway – oh for those halcyon days
of steam!

Come 1867 the world came a-calling with
500 wagons ordered by India; this was
followed with Russia and Argentina waving
their order books. By 1887 the company
became the Gloucester Railway Carriage
and Wagon Company Ltd (GRCW). The
most luxurious coach, people say, that was
ever built was for the Maharajah Holkar of
Indore in 1936.

But the world was in a state of upheaval
and he was given the order of the boot and
fled to the Punjab before he could enjoy it.

In 1868 a profitable relationship began with
Tsarist Russia. Railways were the lifeblood
of this vast kingdom stretching from Europe
to China and Japan. A Gloucester Wagon
Company-supervised works was opened in
Riga (now Latvia), and the stock was sent
out in kit form although it soon closed due
to the sub-standard labour. The first Russian
customer was the Orel and Vitebsk Railway;
a quarter of a million pounds of special axle-
grease had to be delivered with the finished
rolling stock as the regular grease was
poisonous when eaten by the starving
Latvian peasants!

Now if you thought James Bond drove the
original land-to-sea vehicle, not so! In1894
the 'Gantry Car' built for the Brighton and
Rottingdean Seashore Railway Company
stood 40 feet tall on metal legs allowing
it to run through the sea.

The coach body featured a ship's bell and lifeboat and needed a sea captain to drive it, sail it – whatever!

The great little railways of Wales are a legend and a massive tourist attraction for the principality. A classy directors' saloon was built for the narrow gauge Padarn Railway which closed in 1961 but was reincarnated in the 1970s as the Llanberis Lake Railway in English but in Welsh/Cymraeg Rheilffordd Llyn Padarn. It runs in the most stunning scenery around the base of Mount Snowdon. Also in 1896 alongside the GWR Gloucester Central station, the new Gloucester Eastgate station was opened; it ran south to Bristol via Tuffley but closed in 1975.

Another landmark for Gloucester came in 1897 when it built a futuristic Monorail carriage for 'Behrs Lightning Express Railway' to run at the Brussels Exhibition.

So impressed was the King of the Belgians that he ordered a saloon body on a Daimler motor car chassis from the Gloucester Wagon Works!

And if that wasn't prophetic enough, hows about this in 1898 when the company produced an electric taxi for London Electric Cab Company? Over a century ahead of its time, now green eco electric prototypes cars are all the rage to help slow down climate change.

As Victoria's reign came to a close Britain was fighting the Boers and many horse-drawn ambulances, amongst other things, were built for the British Army in South Africa, including the HQ wagon of the Commander-in-Chief, Field Marshall Lord Roberts, which was converted from an ambulance. This was displayed in Gloucester after the war was over but Lord Roberts was so attached to it he kept it.

As war in South Africa subsided so in 1903 it was back to business for GRCW who were now asked to construct a real weirdo: a one-wheeled carette (similar to an open-topped sedan chair) for the use of the Crown Agent for the British Colonies. Stanley Baldwin, the Conservative Prime Minister of the 1920s and 30s, joined the board of directors in 1906. Another sign of the times in 1908 put Gloucester at the forefront of public transport to come with the building of double-decker buses, the first built for Chelmsford, Essex.

In 1914 war was declared, and one month after in September the company struggled to finish an order for Argentine grain wagons as workers responded to the nation and signed on for the Great War. Key men in reserved occupations couldn't be held onto as in WWII. The western front was filled with Gloucester-built stretchers, ambulances, shells and wagons for the French Railways. By the Treaty of Versailles, 821 GRCW workers had been killed.

After the war the Government let the company keep some of its profits to build a sports ground in Tuffley Avenue. Later known as the Winget Ground and nowadays as Tuffley Park it is where Gloucester Cricket Festival was held for many years.

Back to biz again in 1919 when London Transport ordered underground trains for its District Line which runs from the City of London out into the Middlesex suburbs to the west and Essex in the east. LT must have been happy with the goods as in 1931 the Piccadilly Line was to receive Gloucester-built tube trains.

World War II was declared in 1939 and Gloucester produced important armaments such as wooden shoe soles, tank-carrying railway wagons, anti-aircraft projectiles, copper bands, bomb lifting cradles, stampings for tanks and aircraft, Bailey Bridges and spitfire propellers for airscrew experts ROTOL in nearby Cheltenham. GRCW had the finest stock of timber at their disposal during the war and Queen Mary paid two official visits to the Wagon Works during this time. Hopefully she didn't ask to take one home which was her usual habit when she visited people! In July 1941 the first of 764 Churchill tanks rolled off the platform, weighing 45 tons and powered by a Vauxhall flat-12 engine. The Churchill began with a two-pounder gun but was later capable of firing 25lb shells. 'Whale' pivoting sections for Mulberry Harbour used on D-Day were also built at Gloucester.

On 3rd May 1955. Her Majesty Queen Elizabeth II was shown around the Wagon Works with Prince Philip. By the 1950s/60s orders were on the wane and the last wagon to be completed was in 1968, after such an illustrious history. In 1986 the company was taken over and in 1989 some buildings were pulled down to make way for a giant toy shop and the rest of the works was the terra firma for the Peel Centre. Thankfully the impressive main entrance building remains as a go-kart centre; well at least it carries on the tradition of wheels!

As well as the GRCW Archives held in Alvin Street and two Gloucester-built wagons on show at the National Waterways Museum, a 1950s diesel multiple unit is preserved at Pontypool and Blaenafon, Monmouthshire. The original wooden station based at Cinderford, Gloucestershire built by Messrs Eassie, later absorbed by GRCW in 1875, is now preserved on the Dean Forest Railway at Norchard – *www.deanforestrailway.co.uk/ station_norchard.html*

And here endeth another tale of Gloucester.

Gourmet Gloucester

Gloucester Old Spot

It was one lunchtime at my usual restaurant at Staines, Middlesex in the early 1990s that my eyes first alighted upon Gloucester Old Spot; the Specials board announced – 'Gloucester Old Spot Pork Chop'. I ordered it and the succulent meat with a border of crispy fat – don't heave, the fat gives the flavour – meant I was reduced to spending the rest of my culinary life looking for Old Spot whenever pork was a part of my menu.

I got it regularly many miles from Gloucester at a butcher in Lytham, Lancashire. With family living in Blackpool I was able to bring home ample Old Spot supplies. Funny how joints of meat once thought of as cheap are so chi-chi with top chefs now. How often nowadays is pork belly given star à la carte billing as though these culinary celebrities were the first to discover its beauties?

Around the country and in Gloucester itself there are many butchers selling Old Spot meat, including sausages and pies – that is how popular it has become since this poor old pig nearly died out. Needless to say when I returned from the city a couple of months before completing this book I was clutching two loins and three bellies from Morgan's of Westgate Street.

This little piglet has come on in leaps and bounds in the great scheme of piggy things. 1913 seems to be the agreed date pedigree records were first kept and yet in this short span it has become the oldest pedigree spotted pig in the world. The origin of the breed is unknown but is most probably from a mix of the Gloucester native stock with various breeds. They started their porcine rise to being a porky favourite first in the Vale of Berkeley, not far from the city.

In 1855, William Youatt tells in his book *The Pig* 'There is a native stock in Gloucester of an unattractive dirty white colour', but no mention of spots! HD Richardson in *The Pig – Its Origins and Varieties* writes 'it comes from crossing the original Gloucester pig – a large, off-white variety with wattles hanging from its neck, with the unimproved Berkshire, a sandy-coloured prick-eared pig with spots'. Writer William Marshall confirms this in *The Rural Economy of Gloucestershire* way back in 1780.

Why has Old Spot become such a delicacy in such a short time? One big clue is that they are the traditional breed that roamed the apple and pear orchards of Gloucestershire. They were traditionally known as the Orchard or Cottage Pig as they lived in gardens and smallholdings and were reared largely as domestic animals. So when they went scrumping for apples – probably Gloucestershire's own winter russet Ashmead's Kernal – in the orchards they built up a natural reservoir of apple sauce inside, and what goes best with pork apart from apple sauce? Cider!

True Gloucester Old Spots are recognised by the large jet-black spots on their backs and soft floppy ears. Local folklore claims the spots are bruises caused by the avalanche of apples falling on them as they snuffle around sniffing out windfalls. Like their Italian cousins who hunt for truffles the Old Spots love a good forage and graze, picking up all sorts of goodies from the ground. They also lap up the whey left over after the butter and cheese has been made.

Before war was declared against Germany in 1914 Kaiser Wilhelm II, Queen Victoria's grandson, ordered two pigs to be sent to him, but they never made the trip. After the First World War with the rise of modern agricultural methods farmers tried to breed out the pigs, mainly because they did not adapt to the indoor pens introduced post war, and by the 1950s this large, lazy, amiable pig was on the point of extinction before it even had time to reach its centenary.

We now have to cross the county line into Worcestershire where farmer George Styles was so alarmed by the decline of his favourite porker that he set out single-handedly to save the breed. St George, saviour of the Old Spot. Thanks to George, 'grandfather' of this rare breed, the Old Spots are now thriving all over Britain.

However, be on the lookout for lurking interlopers sporting blue and grey spots; they are the result of previous inter-breeding but only jet-black spots will do for a true Old Spot! Oh and do you know some people even tried to get rid of the spots altogether? They said it was because it was harder for butchers to clean up and sell as customers did not want a polka-dot meat. Thankfully, this is a trend that has been reversed. An Old Spot without spots is like zebra without stripes!

The sows make excellent moms, produce plenty of milk and thrive outdoors. Their independence and ability to produce healthy litters twice a year ensures they are fast becoming Britain's favourite organic pig. Gloucester's Folk Museum has an annual Old Spot-fest where you can visit the pigs in their pens and pat the stuffed Gloucester cow too! There is a great picture of an Old Spot in the museum, depicted as a huge fluffy pink ball of a candyfloss pig with black spots held up by four of the tiniest tippy-toe trotters.

The King of England and The Queen of England were two very royal pigs exported to America and used to develop the Spotted Poland China, and others were used to develop the Minnesota No.3 breed. In the mid-1990s, twenty examples of the breed were exported to the USA to help re-establish the Old Spot in its purest form.

Even the Falkland Islands, known more for sheep than swine, have taken delivery of their own Old Spots. And to show how much a prime porker could bring back in 1994, a Gloucester Old Spot became the most expensive pig in the UK. The exotically named Foston Sambo 21 sold at auction for £4000 guineas, that's about £4,200.

Now that's one helluva hog!

Gloucester Cheeses

As a kid I recall seeing a poster in our grocers with pictures of slabs of British cheeses plastered all over a map of the UK. One of them was Double Gloucester and I wondered why it was Double Gloucester? You couldn't get any in the Middlesex area in the 1960s as Gloucester cows were a rarity in Gloucestershire so chances of getting any around Uxbridge were highly unlikely. And it is this particular breed that has the special quality of milk to make the very best of this variety.

During my final research tour to Gloucester, Deana, a friend from British Publishing and Gloucestershire born and bred, made a discovery: she found proper Double and Single Gloucester cheese for sale in the city. It is that same cheese I have perched seductively in front of me now. It is hand-made by Mrs Diana Smart of Old Ley Court, Churcham – about four miles west of Gloucester – using milk from her herd of Brown Swiss, Holstein and Gloucester cows.

Diana has provided the presentation cheeses to the winners of the great Gloucestershire and British tradition of the Annual Cheese Rolling on Whit Monday at Cooper's Hill, Brockworth (about four miles southeast of the city) since 1988, and she is currently the only person in Gloucestershire making the Double Gloucester cheese by hand using traditional methods.

Put away the plastic cheese you buy in supermarkets as I am told most of the Double Gloucester found wrapped in plastic is only that bright orange colour due to food dye, annatto to be precise.

The secret is to take the cheese out of the fridge and bring it to room temperature, say about half an hour before eating.

So here is my verdict – first the Double Gloucester, which is made when there is a surplus of milk and from two lots of the very best of it using the creamiest morning's milk with some from the evening. It is at its peak between May and September. This method produced a long-lasting, dry cheese so it could be kept through the winter or sold at market. There is a little crust on the rind on mine due to the ripening, the colour is a pale orange and the flavour is, wait for it as I am doing this tasting whilst I am writing . . . it is very tangy and much stronger than I was prepared for, this will be perfect for my mum who loves a cheese with bite.

Now for the Single Gloucester: this raw milk cheese doesn't need ripening and comes from either the morning's milk or skimmed evening milk, and is best enjoyed when it is between 9 and 16 weeks old. The farmer's wife kept this for her family. I'm told that in the days when she used to make butter and cream the milk that was left over was less fatty so not good enough for a big bold cheese that matured with age like the Double, which is why the Single was made. So Mrs Farmer kept it for the home. Currently when low cholesterol has become a part of healthy living the Single Gloucester is more popular for the diet. How things change, in days of yore it was for that very reason it was less attractive and popular, and thought altogether a more inferior cheese. Every cheese has its day!

Tasting the Single now . . . hey this is so much more me, smooth and nutty, redolent of Emmenthal, the famous Swiss cheese, perhaps not so surprising as Mrs Smart uses some very pretty Swiss cows in her herd. Another cheesy taste that comes to mind is the Norwegian Jarlsberg, because of its distinct walnutty flavour. This is delicious and I am keeping it all for myself.

Both these cheeses are now out of fashion mainly because of the decline of the Gloucester cow; you can see a very large stuffed one at the Gloucester Folk Museum. It is a fine looking beast, a dark chocolate brown with a custard and cream-coloured rear-end.

It is possible to use milk from other cows to make these cheeses which is probably what some manufacturers do, but their milk will probably be fattier than that from the Gloucester which means you don't get the same texture, taste and colour. I bet this is a fab cheese for cooking, let's see – I think it will give a whole new meaning to cheese on toast – hang on, I will report back.

Yes, I was right, truly scrumptious, melted like a dream and with some thin slices of onion and tomato it made a great snack attack.

If you want to get some of Mrs Smart's Double or Single Gloucester cheese then pop on the web and get her to send you some. She might have to rear a few more Gloucester cows if we create a demand!

For more information go to the website: *www.smartsgloucestercheese.com*

Gloucester Drink

Not being one to kid you, kind, dear reader it would be wrong of me to write with false expertise or gay abandon about drink. Food is most definitely my suite but not beer and ale, so with that I will hand over the tankard to my trusty partner, Doug Beaumont, who will present to you his findings on the real stuff which I am told puts hairs on your chest, so I don't know how mine got there! Here's mud in your eye!

The Dick Whittington Pub

The Dick Whittington Pub, found in Westgate Street and named after the famous thrice-times Lord Mayor of London and one-time resident of Gloucester, has only been a hostelry for a surprisingly short period of time. Although the impressive timbers of the building date back to medieval times, the house has only been open to the imbibing public for a few short years.

Nevertheless, it was the ancestral home of the Whittington family and thus lays just claim to its name. The Dick Whittington's staff are a friendly and welcoming bunch who always have time to welcome newcomers and explain a little about their pub and the wonderful selection of real ales on offer.

For those of us who like spirits, keep an eye out for a hunched figure seen walking around the cellar and for the strange lights seen floating and flitting over the bar, no doubt above the real ale pumps! It is said that furniture moves by itself around the building, which will be a boon to the cleaners, and oft times a ghostly man wearing a flat cap has been seen in and around the bar, probably clutching a glass of one of the following great brews . . .

I will start with the most local of brews and names!

Old Spot 5% brewed by the Uley Brewery, a small independent brewery based in Dursley, Gloucestershire. They offer excellent ales such as Old Spot Prize Ale, Pigs Ear, Hogshead and their strongest, Pigor Mortis! Old Spot is a well-marketed and well-produced beer with a light and enjoyable flavour. Well structured and undemanding, it's a pleasant pint for all occasions.

Monster Ale 4.4% brewed by the Wye Valley Brewery, which is a family-run business started in 1985 by former Guinness brewer Peter Amor. The following year the brewery moved into the old stable block of the Barrels pub in Hereford where they stayed for 16 years, steadily increasing sales and production until no further expansion was possible. In 2002, the brewery moved to its present site in Stoke Lacy, and it is now recognised as the leading cask ale brewery in Herefordshire.

Monster Ale is brewed using pale malt with roast barley to give this dark and rich porter a memorable brew. Wye Valley are also known for their renowned Dorothy Goodbody range of beers and the perfectly palatable Butty Bach, rightfully lauded as overall champion three times running at the CAMRA Welsh Beer Festival.

Golden Braid 3.5% brewed by Hopdaemon Brewery in Newnham, Sittingbourne, Kent. A light-golden, perfect session beer. Flavoursome and quaffable. This is a gentle beer with a frivolous taste that won't give you the morning-after feeling unless you overdo it.

Otter 3.6% brewed by the Otter Brewery established by David and Mary Ann McCaig. The brewery is located on a 16th-century farm in east Devon and produces over 52,000 pints per week. The Otter Brewery has developed a very popular West Country brand and is currently supplying over 450 free trade outlets, 3 national wholesalers and all the major national pub groups.

Tribute Ale 4.2% brewed by St Austell Brewery which has grown steadily since its inception in 1851 to become one of the largest private companies in Cornwall. Still independent, still family owned and a truly regional brewer, St Austell Brewery is part of the fabric of the south west. The well-balanced and complex Tribute Ale is best described as floral, scented and orange with citrus hops and hints of tropical and summer fruits and possessing a clean bitter finish.

Chocolate Stout 4.5% brewed by Dark Star Brewery. Dark Star is a small brewery in Hayward's Heath, Sussex. It has just three tied houses but distributes its fine ales and beers to many other pubs in Sussex and throughout Britain. All stouts are dark brown to pitch black in colour thanks to the use of roasted barley which lends a dry character to the beer as well as a huge roasted flavour that can range from burnt to coffee to chocolate. The 4.5%

Chocolate Stout has a lugubrious, liquorice tang which complements the well-structured and deliberate flavours combining with a long and satisfying finish.

Dark Ruby 6.0% brewed by the Sarah Hughes Brewery. Brewing commenced at the Beacon Hotel, Sedgeley, Staffordshire in the 1860s. By the middle of the 20th century, the pub and brewery were owned by Sarah Hughes. Brewing ceased in 1950 but was restarted in 1988 by Sarah's grandson, who chose to name the brewery after her. The plant consists of an eight-barrel tower-style brewery. Dark Ruby has a thick head and so will you if you drink too deeply of Ruby's delights. It is complemented with a big fresh British hop aroma combining fruity with caramel flavours. Ruby has a big body, richly malted, fairly bitter with a big hop flavour and a toasted, roasted hint in the dry, hop finish.

The New Inn

Visitors to Gloucester and pilgrims to the tomb of King Edward II made a beeline for the 'New Inn' in Northgate Street. The Inn was originally built *circa* 1430 or even earlier and then rebuilt in 1455. About 100 years later it was reputed to be the largest hostelry in England and remains one of the country's finest galleried inns. It remains an impressive and inviting edifice to this day.

Famous visitors reputed to have dropped in to the New Inn include William Shakespeare. From the gallery the seventeen-year-old Lady Jane Grey was proclaimed Queen of England by a royal herald hotfoot from London. She managed to hang on to the crown for a full nine days before the newly proclaimed daughter of Henry VIII, Queen Mary, dealt decisively with her as an early forerunner of the new kids on the block!

Other attractions include a Corsican Fairy, a Mermaid and some waxworks which could all be seen at the New Inn for six old pennies. Eerily visitors to the New Inn

have reported noises in the courtyard and glasses and bottles moving around together with a Queen-like flitting figure in a long robe opening chamber doors!

The cosy friendly ambience of the Inn is mirrored by the locals who all seemed to have time for a chat and time to offer advice about the various brews on offer.

Let's start off with another local:

Saxon 3.8% brewed by Battledown Brewery situated on the edge of Battledown, Cheltenham. Battledown use only the finest country ingredients, floor malted barley, mainly Maris malts, first Gold, Fuggles hops. Saxon is a great session ale with a sharp but smooth bitter taste and a clean, clear nose; the lingering aftertaste is full of hops, well rounded and mellow. Battledown's Saxon is well worth seeking out and will reward the discriminating beer aficionado.

PG Steam 3.9% brewed by the RCH Brewery in Weston-Super-Mare, Somerset. The brewery started in the early 1980s, purchased by the Davey Family in 1984.

The beer's name comes from Paul Davey and Graham Dunbavan – the brewers – and the steam from a steam boiler used to heat the copper. This intriguing multi-layered ale has a flowery, hoppy tang to the nose with medium-bodied hop, bitter taste with a measure of fruit and sweetness.

Fog on the Tyne 4.1% brewed by Northumberland Brewery. In 1997 the brewery opened its ecologically friendly premises at Earth Balance. Other new beers have followed such as Reivers and the very popular Strawberry Blonde along with a range of seasonal beers such as Santa's Secret. The latest to be added to the range are Holy Island Ale and Golden Lab. 'Fog on the Tyne' is a pale, light session ale bursting with hop flavours that's clear in the glass, fresh to the palate and eminently quaffable. It's one of the Northumberland Brewery's regular ales so keep a weather eye open for this one.

The Old Bell

An interesting first-floor pub which can only be accessed via a staircase which might be a little off-putting for seasoned imbibers to negotiate after sampling the brews the Old Bell has to offer. A capacious dining and function room and staircase give entrance to a smaller bar area overlooking Southgate Street. The Old Bell has a Jacobean timber frontage and was originally the home of Thomas Yates, an apothecary. In the first floor bar is an elaborate fireplace with a richly decorated overmantel bearing the date 1650.

The Bell Inn was immortalised by Henry Fielding in his novel *Tom Jones* published in 1749 so is a justifiably popular watering hole especially with those looking for a fun-filled bawdy night out. Noted by some for its real ales, there was only Battledown's Cat's Whiskers available at our visit. But this is notable ale of reasoned quality and one which should definitely be tried by the discerning seeker looking for a memorable drink.

I only had time to try the brew in three historic Gloucester hostelries but I daresay you can find many of the real ales written about in many pubs and clubs in the city, the shire and across the country. I hope you enjoy tasting some of the pints described as much as I did!

Gloucester Stars

Gloucester Cathedral

The Choir – 1995. This mini-series, based on Joanna Trollope's novel, explores the internal politics and scandals of a British cathedral choir school.

Harry Potter and the Philosopher's Stone – 2001. Adventures of J K Rowling's young wizard. The film was set in many mystical locations including the cloisters at Gloucester Cathedral. The best scenes of the cloisters in the film are when Harry fights the troll in the girls' toilets and the scene when Harry and his Gryffindor classmates are led to their dorm for the first time. The pupils of King's School in Gloucester were used for extras in the movie; you see them exiting the cloisters and entering the cloister garden in the film.

Followed by **Harry Potter and the Chamber of Secrets** – 2002.

Gloucester City Centre

Berkeley Square – 1997. Costume drama series about three nannies in Edwardian England.

Animal Ark – 1997. Based on the popular book series by Lucy Daniels starring vet's daughter Mandy Hope and her best friend James Hunter. They both love animals and together they go through many adventures rescuing animals in their home village of Welford.

Cider with Rosie – 1998. The TV adaptation of Laurie Lee's novel of his life in Slad starred Juliet Stevenson. A house in St Michael's Square was used in some scenes and a horse-drawn carriage was filmed going around the Square.

These Foolish Things – 2004. Filmed at the Olympus Theatre, Barton Street and starring Lauren Bacall and Anjelica Huston. A young actress seeks to follow in her famous mother's footsteps.

Outlaw – 2007. A new movie which has partly been filmed in the streets of Gloucester about a group of people that take the law into their own hands and try to right what they see as wrongs in the UK today. Starring Sean Bean and Dannie Dyer.

Gloucester Docks

The Onedin Line – 1972. Series about a young man's rise to wealth and power through the establishing of his own shipping line in the late 19th century.

Maurice – 1987. The life of a Cambridge homosexual – from a semi-autobiographical novel by E M Forster.

Hannay – 1988–89. Adventures of John Buchan's officer-adventurer, Richard Hannay, starring Robert Powell, made famous by Robert Donat in *The Thirty Nine Steps.*

Martin Chuzzlewit – 1994. The main theme is selfishness, portrayed in a satirical fashion using all the members of the Chuzzlewit family. The novel is notable for one of Dickens' great villains, Seth Pecksniff, and the nurse Mrs Gamp.

Buffalo Girls – 1995. In the last days of the Wild West, Calamity Jane works as a mule skinner for Custer, has a fling with Bill Hickok, and tries to reclaim her daughter when she travels to London with Buffalo Bill's Wild West Show. Meanwhile, her best friend, Dora DuFran, a whorehouse madam, deals with domestic and romantic entanglements.

Vanity Fair – 1998. The story of Becky Sharp – determined to scale the heights of society at any cost.

Amazing Grace – 2007. Based on the true story of William Wilberforce, a British statesman and reformer from the early part of the 19th century. Starring Ioan Gruffudd and Albert Finney.

Gloucester Sports

I toyed overnight before writing this segment as I wasn't sure it was wise in a world that can be notoriously flaky and clubs can come and go whether to bother as it would immediately put the book out of date.

But being a sports fan I decided that any book on Gloucester would not be complete without some kind of guide and certainly any guide to this great city cannot NOT mention one of the greatest and most successful clubs in the country, definitely Europe and maybe the world: Gloucester Rugby Union Football Club.

For those of you who aren't into the oval-shaped ball game then Gloucester would be the equivalent to say Manchester United, Chelsea or Glasgow Rangers in soccer terms or the LA Dodgers or New York Yankees in baseball – that is how mega they are. It is a rarity to find any British city where rugby rules the roost and football comes a definite second, but that is certainly the case here in Gloucester.

The club was founded in 1873, so its pedigree stretches forward for well over a century. Massive changes in the game came in the 1970s with the intro of a national cup competition and in 1987/8 a league was given the go-ahead. Finally in the late 1990s the professional game came to Kingsholm – better late than never as it was a case of change or die. This was the case with many famous clubs, with some going back to square one and re-emerging as amateur sides and some that went to the wall; not so for Gloucester who weathered the storm of transformation to come out looking shinier and brighter than ever.

Gloucester's colours are red and white and their nickname is the Cherry and Whites, which kind of belies their renowned toughness on the field, led by their fanatically loyal supporters called The Shed. However, it should be underlined that rugby supporters are much, much more in control than some round-ball soccer fans where anything can happen and sometimes it does!

If I have to take issue with anything Gloucester RUFC has produced then it is the ghastly new club badge that was put together like a police identikit producing the ugliest mug in the heraldic line-up, matched only by Fulham FC! For a club that plays on the incredibly ancient site of Kingsholm Palace and whose ground bears its name then any image or logo should have been given much more thought; I am at their service!

Kingsholm has been their home ground since 10th October 1891and has a fantastic history all of its own and is covered copiously here in my kind of Gloucester. This top-notch club's achievements are far too many to mention but you can get the low-down on their website: **www.gloucesterrugby.co.uk**

To show the strength in depth of rugger in the city there is a Gloucester Women's RUFC and four other clubs that rank in the English Rugby Union pyramid: Gloucester All Blues; Gloucestershire Constabulary; Gloucester Civil Service; Gloucester Old Boys and to add to the blanket love there is for the game in Gloucester, there is an amateur rugby league club called the Gloucestershire Warriors.

Choosing the city's top club and sport was easy but now I am in a quandary as to which is more popular, skittles or football? No I am not being facetious, the traditional game of skittles is massive and at the last count there were nearly 30,000 (yes, thousand) skittles players who probably play team sports or support Gloucester rugby on the side! There is even a local split with Gloucester's arch-sporting rival Cheltenham (more a soccer town!) for in the Spa town skittles is played with either a team of twelve (winter skittles) or six (summer skittles). Each player plays six hands of three balls. However, in Gloucester, the players play ten hands of three balls, and a team is made up of ten skittlers. Skittles are played in pubs, clubs, holiday villages, hotels, in fact anywhere you can get an alley – I have played it in a farm's barn – and there is an annual British Skittles Championship, blessed with colourful team names like the Hillbillies, Fraggles and my particular fave Muhammad Alley Cats. This game is a blast from the past that has grown in popularity rather than faded away.

It is time for soccer – or football – you choose. Gloucester City Association FC originally took to the field in March 1883 as Gloucester YMCA and it wasn't until 1925 they became City. So maybe they haven't set the world on fire but they are still afloat during a time when the professional game has gotten so greedy that it has sucked the life out of the smaller clubs. Nicknamed the Tigers, probably due to their yellow and black striped kit, it isn't easy running a football club in this day and age when one star player in the Premiership would probably keep the whole Gloucester City club running for decades. My hat goes off to people who put their hands in their pockets and heart into volunteering their time for good old clubs, like City, who carry the name of their community into league and cup games all around the country. I know, I have been there, so I salute the officials, fans and supporters of the Tigers for keeping on going against all the odds. One of their honours caught my eye – for the 1981–82 Southern League Cup Final the Tigers lost 2–1 to one of my own Middlesex clubs, Wealdstone, who included future England captain Stuart Pearce in the team, and I am their Patron!

It's nice to note that one of the most famous cricketers ever, Gloucestershire CCC hero WG Grace, refereed one of the football club's earlier matches against Bristol Rovers, in those days called Eastville. Gloucester City is one of the longest-surviving members of the Southern League, a high-up and important rung of the FA National League system. For more information go to the website: ***www.gloucestercityafc.com***

In cricket the main local flag is flown by Gloucestershire County Cricket Club although they tend to play most of their matches at Bristol, venturing out every so often for special festivals. The Gloucester City Winget Cricket Club flies the club cricket flagette in the West of England Leagues closely followed by Kingsholm CC. For more information go to the website: ***www.gloscricket.co.uk***

As befits a city of note like Gloucester it is a centre for many sports, popular, diverse, extreme and here are some to choose from:

Gloucester Athletics Club

Gloucester City Hockey Club

Team Gloster Basketball Club

Gloucester City Cycling Club

City Amateur Swimming Club, Gloucester

Gloucester & Severnside Bowling Club

Gloucester Boardriders

Gloucester Canal Angling

Gloucester City Bowling Club

Gloucester Harlequins CC

Gloucester Clay Shooting Club

Gloucester Martial Arts Centre

Gloucester Rowing Club

Gloucester Ski Centre
(that's right on Robinswood Hill)

Gloucester Table Tennis League

Gloucester Skating Club

Gloucester Golf Club

Gloucester Badminton Club

Gloucester Yacht Club

Severn Athletic Club

Arcadians Cricket Club

Glevum Tennis Club

Glevum Utd FC

Glevum Target Club

Glevum Archers

Gloucester Canoe Club

Gloucester Meteors Ten Pin Bowlers Club

Cotswold Aero Club (Staverton).

There are going to be many clubs not listed, I know of plenty more soccer clubs but the smaller clubs will come and go, although it should be written that Gloucester is a city with a very strong Youth Football (Soccer) League. There may be clubs for other sports not listed basically because we couldn't find them or they failed to return our E-mails. Most of the clubs listed will have a good programme for disabled sportsmen, women and children too; best to contact Gloucester Tourism to get a contact for your particular sport.

Gloucester Attractions

Gloucester Antiques Centre
www.antiques-web.co.uk
1 Severn Road
Gloucester
Tel: 01452 529716 / 01452 422900
Fax: 01452 307161

Gloucester Antiques Centre makes a fine
day out, with antiques and collectibles of
every description. There is something for
everyone; even those that are not antiques
collectors will find items to decorate any
home. Even collectors of modern items
are catered for.

Atobnop
www.atobnop.com/
123 Hempsted Lane
Gloucester
Tel: 01452 312492
Fax: 01452 520294

Fly aboard single turboprop Cessna 208
G-EELS from Gloucestershire Airport at
Staverton to view castles, bridges, rivers,
hills and other scenic features. Please
ring for full details of prices and times.

Barn Owl Centre
www.barnowl.co.uk/owl/wowl/
wbarnowl.asp
The Tithe Barn
Brockworth Court
Gloucester
Tel: 01452 865999
Fax: 01452 865906

The advancement of conservation of
the Barn Owl and other species of owls
through environmental projects, research,
studies and other such activities that will
enhance public education on the ecology
and preservation of owls. To advance
public education in owl and raptor
welfare and husbandry.

Gloucester Cathedral
www.gloucestercathedral.org.uk/
2 College Green
Gloucester
Tel: 01452 528095
Fax: 01452 300469

This former Abbey Church founded 1300
years ago is now the Cathedral Church of
the Gloucester Diocese. The tradition of
daily worship continues. The Cathedral
contains many architectural features, a
Norman nave with massive columns and
the world-famous early fan vaulting in
the complete glazed cloisters, with its
monks' lavatorium.

Gloucester City Museum & Art Gallery

www.glos-city.gov.uk/citymuseum
www.livinggloucester.co.uk
Brunswick Road, Gloucester
Tel: 01452 396131
Fax: 01452 410898

Treasures from all over Gloucestershire reveal the city and county's early life – dinosaurs' bones, incredible Roman and Anglo-Saxon remains and the amazing Birdlip mirror, and Saxon bagatelle set to name but a few! Discover beautiful antique furniture and decorative arts – with special displays of ceramics, and paintings by well-known artists. An exciting programme of events.

The Dick Whittington Family Leisure Park

www.mohaircentre.net/
Little London, Longhope
About 9 miles from Gloucester
Tel: 01452 831137, Fax: 01452 831731

Fun and education for all the family, particularly toddlers to ten year olds, in 100 acres of parkland including indoor play barn, outdoor adventure play park, pedal zone and mohair goats.

Gloucester Folk Museum

www.glos-city.gov.uk/
Content.aspx?urn=1334
www.livinggloucester.co.uk
99-103 Westgate Street, Gloucester
Tel: 01452 396868, Fax: 01452 330495

Attractive Tudor buildings plus extensions displaying the social history, crafts, trades and industries of the City and County of Gloucester from 1500 to the present. New interactive portal gallery. New cottage garden at the rear. Regular special exhibitions, events and activities. Refreshments, museum shop. Baby changing facilities available. Take special note of the stuffed Gloucester cow, marvellous wall paintings and King Charles I handwritten letter.

Gloucester Guildhall

www.gloucester.gov.uk/events
23 Eastgate Street, Gloucester
Tel: 01452 503050
Fax: 01452 305812

Gloucester's premier arts venue featuring art galleries, cinema and live musical and theatrical performances. The Guildhall's café-bar is a laid-back and peaceful haven just a step away from the hustle and bustle of Eastgate Street.

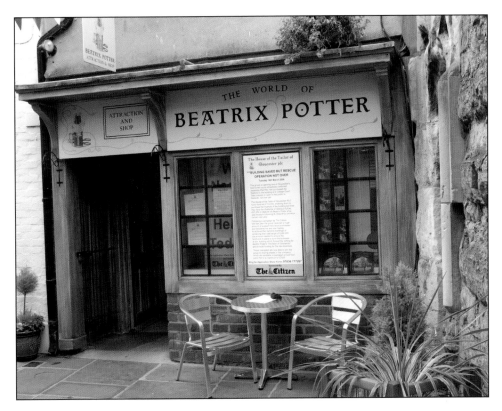

House of the Tailor of Gloucester

9 College Court, Gloucester, GL1 2NJ
Tel: 01452 524914

The little historic house where Beatrix Potter based her illustration for *The Tailor of Gloucester* is down the prettiest walkway close to Gloucester Cathedral. She chose the building and it was painted by her when she visited the city. She used her illustrations together with a local folk tale about a tailor who tried to finish a magnificent waistcoat for the Mayor's wedding one Christmas Day as the basis for the third of her Peter Rabbit books, *The Tailor of Gloucester*, published in 1903. Beatrix Potter later acknowledged this story as her personal favourite.

Sadly the little house had to close for a while in 2006 when the previous owners went bust. But thanks to the infectious enthusiasm of the aptly named Ivan Taylor the locals have been spurred in true community style, and supported by their local newspaper and the Beatrix Potter Society they have rallied to buy the quaint wee house and have now turned themselves into a plc. Even yours truly has done his bit to help save this important part of the great city of Gloucester's heritage and the work of one of Britain's greatest children's author-artists.

This is to whet your appetite, but to finish it off you will have to get in touch with the shop to buy your very special Gloucester based copy . . . happy reading . . .

'In the time of swords and peri-wigs and full-skirted coats with flowered lappets – when gentlemen wore ruffles, and gold-laced waistcoats of paduasoy and taffeta – there lived a tailor in Gloucester.

He sat in the window of a little shop in Westgate Street, cross-legged on a table from morning till dark.

All day long while the light lasted he sewed and snippetted, piecing out his satin, and pompadour, and lute-string; stuffs had strange names, and were very expensive in the days of the Tailor of Gloucester . . .'

Now to support the Beatrix Potter shop in Gloucester make sure you get in touch with them to buy the whole book – it is delightful and you will be supporting a little bit of the city's literary heritage . . .

Llanthony Secunda Priory
www.glos-city.gov.uk/
Content.aspx?URN=1260
Llanthony Priory, Gloucester
Tel: 01452 396620

Park and ruins of Llanthony Secunda Priory, once home to Augustinian canons.

National Waterways Museum
www.nwm.org.uk/
Gloucester Docks, Gloucester
Tel: 01452 318200
Fax: 01452 318202

Located in a listed Victorian warehouse this award-winning museum charts the fascinating 250-year story of our inland waterways. Hands-on interactive, touch screen computers, working models, archive film and historic boats are expertly used to illustrate the characters who made the waterways possible, the technologies used, and what it was like to work and live on the canals.

Nature in Art
www.nature-in-art.org.uk/
Wallsworth Hall
Twigworth
Gloucester
Tel: 0845 450 0233
Fax: 01452 730937

The world's first art gallery and museum dedicated exclusively to art inspired by nature. The collection includes work from 60 countries, spanning 1500 years by over 600 artists and craftspeople. Different artists also working in the studio every week February to November. Gardens and sculptures, children's play area and activities, café.

Queen Boadicea II
www.nwm.org.uk/
Gloucester Docks, Gloucester
Tel: 01452 318200
Fax: 01452 318202

The National Waterways Museum operates boat trips aboard the *Queen Boadicea II* along the Gloucester and Sharpness Canal three times a day. *QBII* is also available for private hire.

Diana Smart's Traditional Gloucestershire Cheese
www.smartsgloucestercheese.com
Old Ley Court, Chapel Lane
Birdwood, Churcham
Gloucestershire GL2 8AR
Tel: 01452 750225
Fax: 01452 750225

Traditional Gloucester hand-made cheese making can be watched every Tuesday and Thursday. On-site sales and mail order.

Robinswood Hill Country Park & Rare Breeds Centre
www.gloucestershire.gov.uk/ index.cfm?Articleid=2145
Reservoir Road, Gloucester
Tel: 01452 303206
Fax: 01452 310633

Robinswood Hill Country Park – one of the finest country parks in south west England – has 100 hectares (250 acres) of Cotswold countryside within 4 km (2 miles) of the centre of the city of Gloucester. Explore the flora, fauna, footpaths and nature trails – giving extensive views of the city and surrounding countryside. Also visit on-site Rare Breeds Farm.

Soldiers of Gloucestershire Museum
www.glosters.org.uk/
Gloucester Docks
Gloucester
Tel: 01452 522682
Fax: 01452 311116

Gloucestershire's military life from the last 300 years including campaigns in Korea, South Africa and Europe.

St James' City Farm
23 Albany Street, Gloucester
Tel: 01452 305728
Fax: 01452 305728

An inner city farm providing a real hands-on contact with farm animals. Rare breeds of pigs, sheep, goats and poultry. Ideal for family visits and school groups. Education room available. Outdoor picnic site.

The Wharf House
www.thewharfhouse.co.uk/
Over, Gloucester
Tel: 01452 332900
Fax: 01452 332901

Exploring 750 years of the Leadon Valley from the Civil War, basketry and willow growing to the ongoing restoration of the Herefordshire & Gloucestershire Canal.

St Oswald's Priory
St Oswald's Road, Gloucester

Ruins of St Oswald's Priory, founded by Aethelred II and Lady Aethelflaed *circa* 890.

Wildfowl & Wetlands Centre
www.wwt.org.uk/visit/slimbridge/
The Wildfowl and Wetlands Trust
Slimbridge
12 miles south of Gloucester
Tel: 0870 334 4000
Fax: 01453 890827

Award-winning visitor centre, wildlife art gallery and observation towers surrounded by thousands of ducks, swans and geese.

Haunted Gloucester

Like so many people I am totally fascinated by the whole aspect of hauntings, ghosties and ghoulies.

As my learned publishers have someone who has made it a lifetime study, obsession even with a particular emphasis on the things that go bump in the Gloucester night, far be it from me to try to out-spook him, so enjoy the next chapter on Haunted Gloucester written by mystery maestro, Mr Paul King . . .

It is perhaps inevitable that in a city as ancient as Gloucester there will be numerous accounts of hauntings. Whilst not wishing to turn the book into a gazetteer of the paranormal, I am going to mention a couple of well-known (to the locals anyway) hauntings. More to the point, I am going to tell you about a personal haunting experience I was privy to some twenty years or so ago.

In the city centre close to Gloucester Cross is an inn named The Old Bell (also mentioned in Gourmet Gloucester). This popular watering hole has made news headlines on more than one occasion due to its alleged hauntings. If ever there was a perfect setting to see a ghost it is here, in this fine Jacobean building tucked away in a corner between shops. The building features an impressively carved fireplace detailing a pictorial history of its former owner, Thomas Yates and his family. The carving bears the date 1650 and as well as featuring the family coat of arms, it also features four cherubs, one of which has six fingers on one hand just like, so it was told, one of his four sons.

The Old Bell Inn has a couple of well-known phantoms – a fastidious spirit known as Elsie, who appears keen to tidy up and re-arrange the cutlery, and a less popular ghost who likes to hurl soap in the gents' toilets – no need for a laxative in there then!

In another part of Gloucester, way back in 1870 a lady named Alice Godfrey found herself face to face with an apparition of a praying monk in the ruins of Blackfriars Priory. She was close enough to see its face and remarked that it had a grey pallor and intense, staring eyes. A much more recent discovery on the same site was that of a skull in what would have been the nave. This was presumed to be the skull of a monk who had died as the result of a head wound. A workman also saw the ghostly monk and another workman also saw him but with blood dripping from a head injury.

My own sighting occurred over twenty years ago. I was born in Matson and many locals know the story of the Blue Lady said to haunt the grounds of Matson House (later called Selwyn School). The story goes that she was fleeing for safety during the Civil War and whilst running, lost one of her shoes. When she went back to retrieve it she was killed in the crossfire. Like most people I suspected that it was just a legend, a product perhaps of someone's overactive imagination.

Until I actually saw her.

Artist's Impression of the Blue Lady

I was out walking my dog, Toby, with my sister Carole back in the early 80s. We were about 50 yards from St Katherine's church between the side entrance to Moat Junior School and the grounds of Matson House and we were walking along the pavement adjacent to the grounds. I was looking into the grounds and it suddenly felt odd, as though time had stopped. I noticed a figure bending down, looking through the leaves, and said to my sister, 'Look at that!' She reacted by running off down the lane with the dog and leaving me alone, staring at the transparent figure of a lady. She was dressed in a pale blue dress, a full dress similar to a ballgown. I recall that it had three quarter length sleeves edged with lace and bizarrely I could see the background of the woods through her. It was as though she was a recording, quite oblivious to me being there. She didn't look up at all and just carried on looking through the leaves.

Was it for her shoe? The odd thing is that there is a blue silk shoe in the Folk Museum and it was found in the grounds of Matson House, along with other artifacts. Could this actually be her shoe? If it is – it's a shame that it can never be reunited with her spirit but I suspect it would not be of any use to attemp a reunion as she is probably what psychics call 'a residual spirit', like a magnetic recording frozen in time and only visible when atmospheric conditions are just right.

After I had seen enough I walked back down the lane and tried to convince my sister to come and see it but she refused point blank. Now, looking back I wish that I had made a note of the date, it was autumn as I recall, probably October but the actual sighting remains as clear as a bell in my head and I feel privileged for seeing it.

One final thing about Matson House. As a boy I remember that one of the upper windows directly opposite St Katherine's had a red mark beneath it in a room where, supposedly, King Charles was in hiding during the Siege of Gloucester. The story goes that he was clipped by a stray bullet whilst looking out of the window and suffered a head wound. His blood stained an area beneath the window and after it started to fade it was touched up with paint every year to keep the story alive. I am not sure if this is the case these days as the place has changed ownership but to a young boy's imagination it was the most thrilling place to be.

Did You Know?

1 Gloucester was at the centre of a number of natural disasters: in 1088 St Peter's Abbey burned down followed in 1089 with the rumblings of an earthquake. On Thursday 22nd May 1102 a great fire struck at St Peter's Abbey and the city itself became a bonfire. Not long after, on Wednesday 8th March 1122 lightning struck St Peter's Abbey's steeple causing a conflagration. On 11th May 1190 a fire turned most of Gloucester to ashes, and in the winter of 1210 the River Severn froze over. The city was again badly damaged by fire in 1214 followed by more flames in 1222/3 with the Lower Westgate area destroyed and the following year Upper Westgate Street as far as College Street became charcoal. The new century 1300 was welcomed with a further fire at St Peter's Abbey and in 1301 Llanthony Priory was hit by fire. 1349 Black Death made a tragic entrance. In 1575 an earthquake damaged Gloucester and in 1604 the plague made another unwelcome entrée. In 1912 the city formed a fire brigade about 900 years too late!

2 Pin-makers were plying their prickly trade in Gloucester according to records since 1396 and by 1802 one in five Gloucestrians were employed in one of nine pin factories. Longsmith Street says it all being the centre of the iron trade – in turn this supply of skilled metalworkers encouraged the later growth of railway, aircraft and other engineering industries.

3 The earliest iron forges go back as far as Roman times if not before to the various early British ages. The metal industry was to form a mega part of Gloucester's long-term prosperity, with everyone from smiths to coopers, goldsmiths to brass pin-makers setting up shop in the city; the first pin-making business was thought to have been introduced by John Tilsley in 1626. Because the River Severn was such an important highway for trade, add hemp and flax-dressing and you have a city that was a hive of activity. To ensure longevity at each stage of its evolution and development, Gloucester cleverly diversified to keep rolling forward with the times and the economic rewards it would bring.

4 England's Glory matches are more than a household name, they have a place in the affections of Gloucester folks. It was all because of Samuel John Moreland – the founder who first started making lucifers (slang for match to light cigarettes) in his small factory in 1867.

Over a hundred years later in 1971, 350 people worked in a factory a few hundred yards from the original site, producing about 12,500 million England's Glory matches annually. Some of the most modern mass production machinery of its type in the world at the time was in constant use in Gloucester. Several match-making factories stemmed from the prosperous timber trade in Gloucester in the 1860s and 1870s. But by 1880 Moreland's was out on its own. Moreland had chosen his location with business acumen close to the Gloucester and Sharpness canal which allowed quick and easy communications. The iconic label features HMS *Devastation* built by the British Royal Navy at Portsmouth in 1871.

5 Gloucester-built Cotton motorcycles enjoyed a number of successes at the famous Isle of Man TT races during the 1920s and 30s but competition from the Far East in the 1960s and 70s brought its demise. Luckily, these light yet strong machines survive in Gloucester Folk Museum.

6 Wall's built Europe's biggest ice cream factory in cool Gloucester.

7 Olbas Oil was developed in Gloucester by G.R. Lane Health Products. The organic fluid which has helped me before many a personal appearance or lecture was given a starring role when Michael Caine was seen sniffing it in the film *Get Carter!*

8 Hubert Cecil Booth patented his first vacuum cleaner, 'Puffing Billy', at the age of thirty after being told by an American inventor that it would be impossible to build a machine that would suck up dust! But born in 1871 he was a visionary and despite early vacuum cleaners being so large they had to be mounted on horse-drawn carts, one of the first tasks was to clean the aisle of Westminster Abbey for the Coronation of King Edward VII in 1901.

9 Twentieth-century excavations near Gloucester Castle, now Gloucester Prison, unearthed the intricately carved Gloucester Tables Set now in the Gloucester City Museum & Art Gallery. This was a game similar to modern backgammon and may have been thrown out by a loser in a fit of pique! Gloucester was also well known for Roberts the toymakers, which made parlour games for Victorian and Edwardian families.

10 Jemmy Wood became a nationally recognised figure as the owner of the Gloucester Old Bank and maybe even Britain's first millionaire. Yet his miserly ways inspired Charles Dickens to create the character of Ebenezer Scrooge in *A Christmas Carol*. The Gloucester Old Bank eventually formed part of today's Lloyds TSB.

11 Born in Westgate Street, Sir Charles Wheatstone invented the electric telegraph and was later knighted for his work in laying the first transatlantic telegraph cable. His Wheatstone Bridge is still used to measure electrical resistance.

ROBERT RAIKES.
FOUNDER OF THE SUNDAY SCHOOL
MOVEMENT.
BORN IN GLOUCESTER, 1735; DIED 1811.
THIRD JUBILEE OF THE MOVEMENT.
CELEBRATED IN 1930.
THIS STATUE.
ERECTED BY CONTRIBUTIONS
AND SCHOLARS IN SUNDAY
LAND, COLLECTED
"THE UNITED
ORGANI

12 Poet W E Henley was born at 1 Eastgate Street in 1849. He lost a leg as a result of a chronic infection of tuberculosis. Although famous for his own poem 'Invictus', he was also the model for his friend Robert Louis Stevenson's character Long John Silver in *Treasure Island*.

13 Born in 1890, Ivor Gurney's brilliant poetry and musical compositions belied an obstinate and unpredictable nature. Following his experiences fighting in France with the Gloucestershire Regiment during the 1914–1918 conflict his war poetry led to ever-deeper personal isolation and depression. He died in 1937 but left such works as 'Songs on Lonely Roads' and 'Severn and Somme'.

14 George Whitefield, born in 1714 at the Bell Inn in Southgate Street, is today better known in America than in Britain. As well as open-air evangelism, he founded 51 seats of learning including Princeton and Pennsylvania Universities.

15 Robert Raikes was baptised at St Mary de Crypt in 1736 and educated at the Crypt School and then the King's School. He was apprenticed to his father, a printer who founded the *Gloucester Journal*. When Dad died he took over and changed its size and layout. He was concerned with the need for prison reform, and used the *Journal* to tell the public of the inhuman conditions inside. As if that wasn't enough he also founded the first Sunday School. He theorised that prisons were full of people who had a deprived childhood, so in partnership with the Reverend Thomas Stock he opened the world's first Sunday School in St Catherine's Street. John Wesley remarked

'I find these Schools springing up wherever I go.' Robert Raikes died in 1811 of a heart attack. The local children who went to his Sunday School attended his burial in St Mary de Lode Church and were each given a shilling and piece of Mr Raikes' plum cake. The original Sunday School was pulled down by Philistines but a statue of Robert Raikes can be seen in Gloucester Park.

16 Originally known as the Music Meeting, the Three Choirs Festival comes to Gloucester once every three years and is shared with Worcester and Hereford Cathedrals. There have been many famous musical personalities associated with the Three Choirs Festival including Edward Elgar who was short of cash so joined the orchestra with his violin!

17 Hammer thrower Lorraine Shaw won a Gold Medal at the 2002 Commonwealth Games held in Manchester.

18 By 1785 Gloucester Castle was hardly existent due to Charles II decreeing its destruction a century earlier. Penal reformer John Howard and county magistrate Sir George Onesiphorus Paul reported that new accommodation for convicts was needed and engaged award-winning prison architect William Blackburn to design a new county gaol which is still in use today and the reason why the Gloucester Prison sits on Gloucester Castle.

19 The glass cover over the East Gate by the Boots store dates from 1980. Since Roman times the D-shaped structure has also served as a prison and a school.

20 The City Museum & Art Gallery was built in 1902 over part of Gloucester's Roman wall. Pop in and you can see it in all its glory down below, well, part of it! But there is much more inside. Look out for amazing fossils, animals, fish – and a range of visiting exhibitions.

21 The martyred Bishop Hooper's Lodgings is home to the popular Folk Museum building. It is a wonderful building dating from 1548 and was once a pin factory – as you will see with some of the most unbelievable exhibits that look more like torture gadgets than pin-making gizmos. It tells the story of Gloucester's remarkable social and economic past – complete with a locally built steamroller.

22 Gloucester City Council's Archaeology Unit is probably unique in being housed in an old fire station – and over a transport museum too! Since it began in 1973 the Unit has unearthed the Gloucester Tables Set and a number of Roman skeletons at Kingsholm.

23 The National Waterways Museum presents the fascinating 300-year-old story of Britain's inland navigations. Located in Llanthony Warehouse in Gloucester Docks since 1988, its exhibits range from traditional 'roses and castles' markings of narrowboats and the very collectable and colourful barge or canal-ware to a rare fireless steam locomotive from Gloucester's wartime power station.

24 Nature In Art is the world's first art gallery and museum dedicated exclusively to art inspired by nature. Superstar contributors include Pablo Picasso, David Shepherd and Graham Sutherland – but there are art courses for enthusiastic amateurs as well!

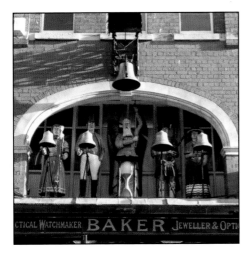

28 I have seen some beautiful clocks both in London and Switzerland but also in Gloucester. The century-old clock over Bakers the jewellers in Southgate Street depicts the four nations of England, Wales, Scotland and Ireland along with Old Father Time. The Mall Eastgate Shopping Centre is home to a spectacular timepiece themed on Beatrix Potter's *The Tailor of Gloucester* story.

29 Lizzie Harker, born in 1863, wrote *Miss Esperance and Mr Wycherley* and its sequel *Mr Wycherley's Ward*; she died in 1933.

25 Based in a historic former seat of local government, the Guildhall Arts Centre offers an amazing selection of installation art and performance, art house cinema, music and other cultural events. Gloucester has dual theatres in the King's and the Olympus, so named because it is home of the Gloucester Operatic and Dramatic Society – the G.O.D.S.!

26 Built on the site of the city's first Victorian public baths, GL1, Gloucester's Leisure Centre, offers every facility for the 21st-century athlete. With state-of-the-art swimming pools and fitness and exercise areas, the centre also boasts a martial arts dojo, events hall, squash courts, a four-lane indoor bowls area, badminton and ball games hall and gymnastics arena.

27 In 1498 St Peter's Abbey (Gloucester Cathedral) built the Fleece Inn to cater for all the pilgrims and visitors coming to the city to worship at Edward II's tomb; he by now had attained cult status.

30 John Taylor, the Elizabethan Water Poet born in 1580, wrote many bawdy and raw pieces and composed pageants for the Lord Mayor of London, Dick Whittington himself perhaps, and also published works about his oscillations!

31 Dick Whittington was born around 1350 in Gloucester to William Whittington, Lord of Pauntley. When he was 13 he was sent to be apprenticed to John Fitzwarren in London. Later he was to become the greatest merchant in the country. He supplied finest silks from China for the wedding dresses of the daughters of King Henry IV and even loaned money to him. He DID become mayor of the City of London four times in fact – 1397, 1398, 1407 and 1420 and just like the fairy-tale promises he married Alice, the boss's daughter. Next time you go to see the pantomime you'll know it really is for real – except for one thing, 'Turn Again Whittington THRICE Mayor Of London,' when it was QUADRUPLE, I guess it doesn't scan as well . . .

Global Gloucester

Back in the days when people took off to the new colonies they would pack up a memory of where they lived along with their goods and chattels.

We all want to belong to somewhere so clinging on to the familiar and what is safe and sound is human nature. What better way to settle down in a strange land than to take something with you that weighs nothing but means everything – your home town name. Although many immigrants exited the British Isles fleeing religious persecution or convicted to be banished to the colonies there were many folks who set out to find fame and fortune of their own volition.

In Gloucester's case it is fascinating to see how the name was transplanted. Some towns were named in honour of whoever held the title Duke of Gloucester at the time; perhaps they had been given a charter by him and wanted to show their appreciation because they knew which side their bread was buttered! Some Gloucesters are direct transplants of the city or county name from the mother country – one was even named from one American colony to another. It is easy to forget that the United States didn't exist until 1776 so before then all the colonies (states) were separate and independent of one another.

See how some of the Gloucester spellings have been changed to make it easier to pronounce; some are spelt as they sound whilst others stick to the traditional way.

There are some Gloucester places where I couldn't find how they were named, despite lots of research. I would be very happy to hear from you in my pursuit of perfection.

Australia

Gloucester, New South Wales
The Gloucester district was first visited by Robert Dawson, Chief Agent for the Australian Agricultural Company in 1826. Settlement occurred in the 1830s. It was not until 1855 that the township of Gloucester was established. The land was first used for raising sheep but it soon became clear that climatic conditions were inclement. Today cattle, dairy farming, timber and tourism have become the major industries.

Gloucester Island, Queensland
The island was declared a National Park in 1993. Just off the Queensland mainland between Airlie Beach and Bowen lies Gloucester Islands National Park, a scenic group of inshore continental islands. Gloucester Island, the largest, is home to a colony of endangered Proserpine rock wallabies. Sandy and coral rubble beaches, rainforest and seclusion are some of this park's main attractions. The islands and surrounding waters are part of the Great Barrier Reef World Heritage Area and are protected.

Canada

Gloucester, Ontario was named after Prince William Henry, Duke of Gloucester (14th November 1743 – 25th August 1805) a grandson of Hanoverian King George II and a younger brother of King George III.

Gloucester was a city in eastern Ontario on the Ottawa River and is now a suburb of the Canadian capital, Ottawa. Gloucester Township was established in 1792. It was incorporated as a township in 1850 and became a city in 1981. Gloucester was one of the 11 municipalities that merged in 2001 to form the 'new' city of Ottawa.

Gloucester, Ontario has its own flag.

Gloucester County, New Brunswick

is located in the northeastern corner of the maritime province and was formed in 1826 from part of Northumberland County. Its capital is Bathurst. The eastern section of the county is known for its Acadian culture. The Acadians are the descendants of the original French settlers scattered throughout parts of the northeastern region of North America. Although Acadians and Quebecers are both French Canadians, Acadia was founded four years prior to the founding of Quebec and in a totally geographically separate area. Furthermore, Acadians to a great extent hail from different parts of France than do Quebecers. Consequently, the two have formed distinct cultures. In the Great Expulsion of 1755, Acadians were uprooted by the British; many later resettled in Louisiana, where they became known as Cajuns.

Gloucester Junction, Bathurst, New Brunswick

A separate community to the south of the city of Bathurst on the right side of the Nepisiguit River.

USA

Gloster, Georgia was established complete with post office in 1893. It was a flag station on the Seaboard Railroad, five miles west of Lawrenceville, and named for an official of the railroad.

Gloster, Louisiana is in De Soto County.

New Gloucester, Maine was

incorporated in 1774 as the 29th town in what was then a part of Massachusetts and only thirty-nine years after sixty inhabitants of Gloucester, Massachusetts petitioned the General Court of Massachusetts for a tract of land six miles square above North Yarmouth. This was granted in 1737 and that same year John Millett was sent to cut a road from Cousin's River in North Yarmouth to the centre of the town. The name New Gloucester was chosen in the hope the town would be to the new settlers what the town of Gloucester, Massachusetts had been to their fathers.

The Shakers came to New Gloucester in 1782/3 led by Elder John Barnes, and the first meeting was held in the home of Gowan Wilson Senior. The Shaker Village was organised in 1791 and the meeting house was built and ready for use on Christmas Day in 1794 and still stands with its original paint gleaming as brightly as it did then. Other buildings soon followed and the community reached its peak in the 1800s. The Shaker community is still active although the number of members has declined through the years.

The Shaker movement is an offshoot of the Religious Society of Friends (or Quakers) which originated in Manchester, Great Britain in the late eighteenth century (1772). Strict believers in celibacy, Shakers maintained their numbers through conversion and adoption.

Gloucester, Massachusetts

Gloucester is America's oldest fishing port. Founded in 1606 and christened Le Beauport by Samuel de Champlain due to its beautiful harbour. The local Indians called it Wingaersheek.

Some years later, in 1614, Captain John Smith travelled from Monhegan Island down the coast ending his journey at Cape Cod. Prior to that, whilst passing the cape of land where Gloucester is now, he named it 'Tragabigzanda' in honour of an Ottoman lass who had befriended him when imprisoned in what we now call Turkey. Captain Smith presented a map of the eastern coast to the son of King James I/VI, Prince Charles who would later become King Charles I. Charles called it Cape Anne after his mother, Anne of Denmark. The name eventually was changed to Cape 'Ann'.

In 1623, men from Dorchester, Dorset County, Great Britain were sent to establish a fishing and trade plantation. The Dorseters established the first permanent settlement of the Massachusetts Bay Colony. The men anchored their ship in the harbour and set up fish-drying platforms on 'Fishermen's Field'. In 1626, they were recalled to Great Britain after three hard, unsuccessful years. Four of the men stayed and were led down the road by Roger Conant to Salem and Beverly. But by 1642, other settlers had arrived at Gloucester. The settlement was formally incorporated that year and called Gloucester due to the large number of settlers from Gloucester, Great Britain and became a city in 1873.

In the American War of Independence, Gloucester sent nearly 300 men to fight against their ain folk – most of who fought at the famous battle of Bunker Hill.

There is separate village called Gloucester Harbor situated in a glorious location on the south side of Cape Ann.

Gloucester competes with the home city in the UK in having a movie career. In Gloucester, UK *Harry Potter* was filmed at the cathedral and in Gloucester, MA the town was at the heart of *The Perfect Storm* starring George Clooney and Mark Wahlberg.

The movie, based on the best-selling book by Sebastian Junger, traces the last trip of the local swordfishing boat the *Andrea Gail*, which was lost at sea during the infamous no-name storm of October 1991.

Gloster, Maplewood, Minnesota
The history of Maplewood goes back about 150 years. Before settlers arrived the land in Maplewood was inhabited by the Dakota Indians. In 1886, the Wisconsin Central Railroad built a line that intersected with the St. Paul and Duluth Railroad. A new town was planned at the junction of these two railroads that was predicted to 'rival St. Paul'. William and Mary Dawson laid out a town and decided to name the place 'Gladstone' after William Gladstone, a popular British statesman of the time. Dawson planned to relocate his plough work business there and was able to entice The St. Paul and Duluth Railroad to put its shops in Gladstone. For a time, the little village prospered. In the 1890s the town employed 1,000 workers. It had a post office, a hotel, at least two saloons, a brothel and a population of about 150.

Gladstone suffered a series of misfortunes that was its demise. First, a fire destroyed the Plough Works. Then the founder of the town, William Dawson filed for bankruptcy. The last straw was when the railroad shut down the shops sometime around 1917. Gladstone became a ghost town with many people leaving or burning their houses for insurance. Trains still remained an everyday sight in Gladstone for many years after. The depot stayed in service through the 1950s but the railroad changed the name to Gloster in 1910 to avoid confusion with Gladstone Michigan.

Gloster, Mississippi is a town in
Amite County. T T Martin, an evangelist and one of the most prominent figures in the anti-evolution movement in the 1920s is buried here.

Gloucester City, New Jersey is part
of the Camden Philadelphia metro area.

Gloucester Furnace, Egg Harbor
City, New Jersey is now a ghost town.
It was a village that supported a bog iron furnace, typical of the New Jersey Pine Barrens. It started around 1813, and closed down around 1848 or soon after. In its heyday there were only about 25 houses there for the workers. Very few people, even local area residents, have ever heard of the place now. The Post Office was in operation 1827–1855. The furnace was started by a cousin of the owner of Weymouth Ironworks, who was also a son of the owner of Batsto Ironworks. There are now just 3 houses in the area. The site is located along a dirt/sand road off County 624 in the northern (mostly uninhabited) part of Egg Harbor City. There are very few, if any, but you may pick up bits of slag and bog iron ore.

Glouster Landing, New Jersey is
near the coast in Atlantic County.

Gloucester Township, New Jersey
The present Township of Gloucester was one of the original townships that comprised Old Gloucester County. It became the county's first political subdivision in 1685. The boundaries of the county extended from the Delaware River to the Atlantic Ocean until 1683, when it was divided into two townships: Egg Harbour Township and Gloucester Township. Gloucester Township, which took its name from the home country's cathedral city of Gloucester, was further subdivided into four smaller townships, and on 1st June, 1695 became one of the first New Jersey municipalities to be incorporated. In 1884, the township became part of the newly formed County of Camden.

Gloucester County, New Jersey
Gloucester County was founded in 1686. During the 1700s, Gloucester County included territory now part of Camden and Atlantic Counties. Woodbury, founded in 1683, is the oldest town in the county. The National Park was the site of the Revolutionary War Battle of Red Bank (now included in a county park) where Fort Mercer once stood. Here you can see the remains of the British ship *Augusta* (stored in a shed in the park) which sank during the battle. During the colonial era Gloucester County's main economic activity was agriculture. In Woodbury (even then the main town) was located the county courthouse, the county jail, a Quaker meeting house (still in existence), and an inn, on the current location of Woodbury Crossings. Smugglers were rife because of the county's many creeks leading to the Delaware River and the Atlantic Ocean.

Gloucester, North Carolina
The first land-grants of the Gloucester-Straits community are recorded as 1713 and 1714. It is listed by the Carteret County Historical Research Association as being the fourth oldest settlement in the county. It is younger than Merimon Township, Beaufort and Harlowe by only six, four, and one years!

Its first settlers moved to unclaimed property along navigable waters. Carteret's early springs and excellent farmland attracted families from other colonies as well as immigrants from Europe. Farming and seafaring provided livelihoods for the majority of families. At one time tobacco was widely cultivated. Commerce never was heavy in the Straits, though Captain Joe Pigott sailed his three-masted *Charmer I* and smaller *Charmer II* to the West Indies and New England for years of coastwise trade early in this century.

In 1910, the section of Straits Township known as Up Straits (although it was down east from Straits Post Office) was granted a post office and another name had to be chosen to avoid confusion between the two. Captain Pigott, who had visited and admired Gloucester, Massachusetts many times in his sailing days, used his influence to have the community named Gloucester.

Glouster, Ohio is a village in the Athens metro area and named after Gloucester in Great Britain.

Glocester, Rhode Island

Glocester (originally 'Gloucester') was established in 1639 just three years after Roger Williams came from Massachusetts due to a battle of religious ideals and founded Rhode Island's first settlement at Providence based on his own more lenient tenets. A number of books of the time record the town's settlement as 1700.

Glocester's coat of arms appears with three red arrowheads divided by three red chevrons upon a golden shield. This device is based on the arms of Gloucester, Great Britain, which uses three red chevrons. The arms of the ancient family of Clare, who were Earls of Gloucester, made the distinction by the addition of ten torteaux ('roundels' or half-circles). In Glocester's arms the torteaux have been changed to three arrowheads to signify that Glocester, Rhode Island is in America but its origins are linked to Gloucester in the mother country.

On 16th March 1730 the Town of Glocester was separated from Providence and organised as the Town of Glocester. It derived its name from Frederick Lewis, Duke of Gloucester, who was the son of King George II of Great Britain. On 16th April 1806, Old Glocester was divided in half, with the southern half retaining the original name and the northern half being called Burrillville.

Gloucester County, Virginia

The history of Gloucester County began soon after the settlement of Jamestown in 1607. Though the county would not be formed until 1651, many events came to pass on these lands that were instrumental to the colony's survival. Some say the county was named for Henry, Duke of Gloucester, third son of King Charles I, others say it was called after Gloucester in Great Britain. Gloucester is pronounced GLOSS-ter in New England, but in Virginia it is GLAW-ster in the British tradition. When British settlers arrived at Jamestown in 1607 the Indian stronghold of Chief Powhatan was located on the north side of the river actual in Gloucester. It was here that Powhatan built his home Werowocomoco. According to legend his daughter, the Princess Pocahontas, saved the gallant Captain John Smith from a tragic death at the hands of the Indians, and thus entered the pages of Virginia's history.

Early land patents were granted in 1639, but it was not until after 1644 that Gloucester was considered safe for settlement. George Washington's great grandfather received a Gloucester County land patent in 1650. Gloucester County was formed from York County in 1651, and consisted of four parishes: Abingdon, Kingston, Petsworth and Ware. Kingston parish became Mathews County in 1791.

In the 1600s and 1700s, Gloucester was a tobacco producing area, and many old plantation homes and magnificent private estates remain today in perfect condition. There are fine examples of Colonial architecture in the churches of Ware (1690) and Abingdon (1755), and some early buildings remain at the county seat on the Courthouse Green still actively serving the public.

Following British settlement, Gloucester became home to many colonial leaders.

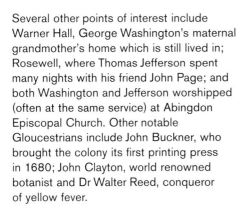

Several other points of interest include Warner Hall, George Washington's maternal grandmother's home which is still lived in; Rosewell, where Thomas Jefferson spent many nights with his friend John Page; and both Washington and Jefferson worshipped (often at the same service) at Abingdon Episcopal Church. Other notable Gloucestrians include John Buckner, who brought the colony its first printing press in 1680; John Clayton, world renowned botanist and Dr Walter Reed, conqueror of yellow fever.

Gloucester's role during the American Revolution was pivotal. The southern tip of the Gloucester County peninsula extends into the York River and is directly across from Yorktown itself. This finger of land, named Tyndall's Point for Captain John Smith's mapmaker, Robert Tyndall, became known as Gloucester Point at the time of the Revolution. A fortification existed here already, built to protect the waterways of Virginia. The British Army refortified the point in August 1781 and British forces occupied the point for much of the War. Gloucester Point is the site of the 'Second Surrender' by General Charles Lord Cornwallis to General George Washington at Yorktown.

The history of the daffodil in Gloucester County, Virginia is almost as old as the county itself. When Gloucester was formed in 1651 from part of York County the early settlers brought these floral reminders of British springtime as they established themselves in the area. The soil and weather conditions were ideal for the daffs. The bulbs were passed from neighbour to neighbour and spread from the gardens of the great houses to grow wild in the fields. Some, such as the hardy Trumpet Major variety, seemed to thrive on neglect. By the beginning of the 20th century daffodils grew at will in the untended fields of Gloucester.

It is from this abundance of natural beauty that grew the extensive daffodil industry which earned the county the title 'Daffodil Capital of America' in the 1930s and 40s.

One interesting area of Gloucester County is known as Guinea. Located near Gloucester Point, the area has historically been the centre of the seafood industry of the county. Whilst the number of participants in this industry has declined over the years, it remains the cultural core of the community. These watermen are known locally as 'Guineamen'. This term is often used as such by residents in other parts of Gloucester County. Guineamen often speak a heavily accented form of English as would be spoken locally in Britain's South of England, but not necessarily a distinct dialect. This is unusual as the rest of Virginia, indeed mid-western American English will sound its 'r's at the end of a syllable or before a consonant.

The name 'Guinea' is of uncertain origin; however, a commonly held explanation is that this area of Gloucester County was named 'Guinea' in an effort to deride the Tories (Loyalists) who quartered Hessian (German) mercenaries in service of the British Crown during the Revolutionary War; these soldiers were paid one Guinea per day. It is believed the Hessians were attached to General Charles Lord Cornwallis' (of Yorktown fame) army and either occupied lower Gloucester during the closing days of the Revolutionary War or deserted their service fighting for the British. What is known is Cornwallis sent British troops and cavalry (under the command of Colonel Banastre Tarleton) to occupy Gloucester in October 1781. Hessians may have been a part of that contingency who were sent to secure lower Gloucester due to its strategic importance at the mouth of the York River.

The Greenway

There are plenty of the usual brands to stay in or around Gloucester but in my pursuit of both 5 star history and luxury I like to nestle in a place where I can pamper myself in comfort and have the joy of the pleasures of yesteryear to look at and listen to.

To this end I discovered the charming Greenway, a country house hotel with an ambience that blends together the Tudor, Stuart and Edwardian eras. Only a few miles out of Gloucester city centre in the village of Shurdington, about 15 minutes' drive on the road to Cheltenham Spa, you find peace in the quiet of the Gloucestershire countryside.

The Greenway was the Manor House of the Lord of Little Shurdington. It was built between 1584 and 1616 during the times of Queen Elizabeth I and King James I/VI

by the then Lord of the Manor, William Lawrence, whose kith and kin came from Lancashire way back at the end of the 12th century.

When he died in 1638, William passed the pile to his nephew, William. Now this could get confusing as nephew William married Anne and they had a son called ... you've got it, William! Son William died when he was just 22, following his mother to an early grave. All three are buried at nearby Badgeworth Parish Church. There is a memorial tablet along with the Lawrence coat of arms.

The Greenway's tranquil gardens remain today very much as they were first laid out way back then in memory of William's beloved wife and son; the Great Oak still stands in the meadow and the Sunken Garden is still a place for contemplation as it once was.

It wasn't until some time in the 1700s that The Greenway (from the Anglo-Saxon 'weg' meaning path, (dirt) road or way) was given the name it is now known by, before then it was called the Little Shurdington Estate. The long, straight, narrow road that leads to the house is part of a pre-Roman path or drover's road that runs up into the hills and the mysterious long barrow. A long barrow is a prehistoric earth mound housing a collective tomb dating back to the Neolithic Age – 4000 BC–2500 BC.

The Greenway stayed in the Lawrence family until 1853 when it was acquired by Roger Fairbridge and following his passing his widow sold it on by auction at the Bell Hotel in Gloucester. Most of the cosy interior dates from Edwardian times: in 1910 the Venerable Archdeacon Sinclair of Hatherley employed Ernest Newton to remodel the house. Newton added the projecting wings on the east front and the long service wing on the north side, and imported the eye-catching mid 18th-century chimney piece in the entrance hall.

In 1946 many aspects of the original house were converted by the Austen family into the country house hotel as it is today.

For you royal lovers, Her Majesty the Queen Mother often stayed at The Greenway when pursuing her favourite hobby, horse-racing at the Cheltenham Gold Cup. I was delighted to present to the management, Von Essen Hotels, the remaining photographs of me with the Queen Mum when I met her back in 1978 at Olympia in London. It was then the British Media blessed me with the honorary appellation, the Astrologer Royal, becoming the first astrologer in 400 years to publicly present to a member of our royal family their astrological charts.

Pay a visit or stay a while and you will be able to see the Queen Mum and me in pride of place adding a little more history to the story of The Greenway – oh and be sure to tell them I told you to call!

For more information go to the website: *www.thegreenway.co.uk/*

Gloucester Information

Media List

Gloucester Citizen
6-8 The Oxbode
Gloucester GL1 2RZ
Tel: 01452 424442
www.thisisgloucestershire.co.uk

Severn Sound
Bridge Studios
The Mall Eastgate Shopping Centre
Gloucester GL1 1SS
Tel: 01452 572400
www.severnsound.co.uk

BBC Radio Gloucestershire
London Road
Gloucester GL1 1SW
Tel: 01452 308585
www.bbc.co.uk/gloucestershire

The British Publishing Company Limited
33 St Michael's Square
Gloucester GL1 1HX
Tel: 01452 418191
www.british-publishing.com
www.russellgrantsgloucester.co.uk

Tourism

Tourist Information Centre
28 Southgate Street, Gloucester GL1 2DP
Tel: 01452 396572
www.visitgloucester.info

Gloucester City Council
North Warehouse, The Docks
Gloucester GL1 2EP
Tel: 01452 522232
www.gloucester.gov.uk